Athens

Front cover: the Acropolis at night

Right: Evzone on guard at the Memorial of the Unknown Soldier

TOP 10 ATTRACTIONS

New Acropolis Museum • A splendid repository for the antiquities of the Acropolis with space for the Elgin Marbles *(page 40)*

The Theatre of Dionysos • It once entertained ancient Athenians. Today the theatre festival venues are unsurpassed *(page 37)*

The Goulandrís Museum of Cycladic Art • See how modern the delightful ancient sculptures seem *(page 64)*

The National Archeological Museum • View masterful treasures, such as this boy jockey from the Hellenistic era *(page 56)*

The Acropolis · Topped by one of the world's greatest cultural monuments, the Parthenon, this is the rock on which ancient Athens was founded *(page 27)*

Pláka · A maze of narrow streets lined with restaurants and neoclassical mansions *(page 40)*

Delphi · Make an excursion to the ancient home of the oracle *(page 78)*

Monastiráki · One of the most colourful parts of the city *(page 50)*

Náfplio · This old port town makes an ideal base for exploring the Argolid *(page 7)*

The Hephaisteion · Considered to be the finest surviving Greek temple in the world *(page 47)*

CONTENTS

34

47

55

32

63

94

INTRODUCTION

Mention the name Athens, and almost everyone will have some preconceived ideas about the city. Socrates painted a verbal picture in the 4th century BC, Pausanias followed suit in the Roman era. Nineteenth-century travellers gave it an air of romance. In the 20th century, the Greek film industry added its own slant to the image with such movies as *Never on Sunday* and *The Red Lanterns*, and schoolchildren still learn about the 12 great gods of ancient Greece.

This small city set on and around a dramatic hill of rock – the Acropolis – became the cradle of Western civilisation. During its heyday in the 5th and 4th century BC, the inhabitants were highly sophisticated in their thoughts and actions, their tastes and fashions. They left an enduring legacy of concepts and ideas for humankind, but they also bequeathed a remarkable number of buildings and artefacts that tell us about their lives. The remains of the temples of the Acropolis are instantly recognisable, and hundreds of statues, along with ordinary household pottery, jewellery and tools exert a fascination on anyone who enjoys exploring the past.

The Modern Capital

The city of Athens is more than a sum of these ancient parts. After Constantinople became the capital of the eastern Roman Empire in the 4th century AD, Athens gradually shrank to little more than a village, only to rise like a phoenix from the ashes after 1834, the year it was nominated the capital of the modern country of Greece. Neoclassical design was fashionable in much of Europe during the mid-19th century, and the impressive buildings then con-

Neoclassical mansions in Pláka

Urban population

Athens is by far the biggest city in Greece. The Larger Urban Zone contains more than four million people, over a third of the country's entire population.

structed in Athens could be seen against their proto-types. The elegant simplicity of the old Parliament Building, the graceful façade of the University, and decoration on the Academy all hark back to ancient examples. In 1923, following the collapse of the Ottoman Empire and Greece's disastrous move into Turkish Anatolia, Greece and Turkey agreed on religiously based population exchange, which brought to Greece more than a million Orthodox Christians, resident in Asia Minor since antiquity. Athens strained to accommodate many of them in the first hastily erected suburbs around the central area. The result is that much of Athens is overbuilt, with congested, narrow streets and a shortage of parking spaces. The Post-World War II policy of *andiparohí* also radically changed the look of the city *(see page 23)*.

New Transport

The heart of Athens, the central, 19th-century triangular grid defined by Sýntagma (Sýndagma) and Omónia squares and the Kerameikos archaeological site, has been rejuvenated with pedestrianised streets, carefully renovated neoclassical buildings and attractive lighting. This triangle, covering the districts of Monastiráki and Pláka immediately south, and the Acropolis just beyond, contains many of the most interesting places to see.

A metro system that is still expanding provides a fast, inexpensive service along three main lines and east of the city out to the new airport, which can also be reached by a new suburban line from the city's main railway station, Stathmós Laríssis. The tram runs south from Sýntagma Square

Metro station at Sýntagma Square

down to the shore at Glyfáda. These systems enable you to reach the major archaeological sites in Athens easily and fast. The Attikí Odós, the new toll road around Athens, allows you to drive easily between different parts of the city, and it will get you to the National Road heading north or west in 10–15 minutes.

If you are heading for the islands, ferries and hydrofoils fan out from the ports of Piraeus and Rafína.

Athenian Way of Life

Athens is a city to be enjoyed. Every district has its own small squares with cafés, where people gather for a drink or meal. You'll be surprised at the wealth of good restaurants offering different national cuisines, many of them in beautiful settings. Despite this, the traditional Greek taverna is still as popular as ever. Locals and visitors alike enjoy the fresh and delicious dishes that have been served for centuries.

Byzantine church of
Kapnikaréa

The Athens Festival, held annually from June to September, offers a full programme of music, dance and theatre at various outdoor venues. Classical music is performed at the indoor Mégaro Mousikís. Sports, largely football and basketball in which the Greeks have been successful in recent years, are also followed avidly.

Tradition still plays an important part in daily life. The family forms the backbone of Greek society and filial ties are strong. Children play safely in the streets with *yiayiá* (grandma) keeping a watchful eye; new babies are proudly shown to the world during the evening *vólta* (stroll). Families gather for a weekend taverna meal, spending a couple of hours in noisy debate (some may say argument) while eating their fill. Greeks are excellent hosts, even in commerical situations such as a taverna – a large party can expect a digestif or token dessert on the house. Shopkeepers are skilled salesmen, though not overbearing.

The Orthodox Church – long the symbolic unifier of the Greek diaspora, and constitutionally an established religion – has seen its influence wane considerably in recent decades. Religious observance remains strongest amongst women and the older generations, who still schedule a stop in the nearest church to reverence an icon or light a candle. But even the sceptical young will still be married in church, and have their offspring baptised there.

Looking to the West

Since joining the European Community in 1981, Greece has moved closer to her Western cousins, and was one of the first wave of countries to adopt the euro. The EU has provided large sums in aid, which has been used to upgrade roads and telecommunications throughout the country. The modern Olympic Games were first held in Athens in 1896, and when the city staged the Games for the second time, in 2004, it provided a stimulus for many infrastructure improvements. The initial cost strained the economy, but within a couple of years the investment was seen to be paying off. Tourism remains Greece's major foreign currency earner, with 11–12 million people visiting each year. People of many nationalities tread the marble steps of the Acropolis to gaze at the birthplace of Western civilisation, finding a city that is more open, lively and accessible than it has been since ancient times.

The Acropolis at night

A BRIEF HISTORY

In ancient Greek mythology Athens was named following a contest between Athena, goddess of wisdom, and Poseidon, god of the sea. Both coveted the city, so it was agreed that whoever came up with the more useful gift for mortals would win. The half-human, half-serpent first king of Athens, Kekrops, acted as arbiter.

First came Poseidon, who struck the rock of the Acropolis with his mighty trident and brought salt water gushing forth. Then it was Athena's turn. She conjured an olive tree, which proved more useful and valuable. Thus she acquired the position of the city's special protector.

Ancient City-State

The real story of the city-state of Athens is just as fascinating. The earliest Athenian settlement, dating from around 3000BC, was built on the Acropolis. During the late Bronze Age, also known as the Mycenaean Period after King Agamemnon's famous city in the Peloponnese, a large palace was built on the Acropolis. For several centuries, the Mycenaeans dominated the eastern Mediterranean and Aegean. A long series of conflicts, however, including the legendary siege of Troy, weakened these mighty mainland warriors.

Around 1150BC waves of Dorians from the north swept into the area. On horseback, armed with iron spears and shields, they overpowered the Mycenaeans and reduced their Peloponnesian strongholds. The ensuing 'dark age', from 1150–750BC, resulted in large-scale migrations of Greeks around the Mediterranean. Palaces throughout the country were destroyed and Greece began four centuries of essentially subsistence existence. When prosperity returned it came with the political structure of the *polis*, the city-state.

The city-state of Athens came to occupy the entire Attic peninsula 50km (31 miles) south to Cape Sounion, northeast to the Rhamnous fortress, and southwest to Mégara, a total of 3,885 sq km (1,500 sq miles). This extensive territory included some highly advantageous natural resources. The broad Mesógia plain was in antiquity and remains today a productive farming area, which was able to support the growing population. The Lávrio mines near Sounion yielded silver; the mountains of Ymittós and Pendéli provided marble for building; and both Pireás and Pórto Ráfti were large natural harbours – factors critical to Athenian strength.

Towards Democracy

Perhaps because of water shortages, Athens developed later than the other city-states, but by the 6th century BC she was a major city. The first steps towards democracy were taken

A vase from the 6th century BC

early in the 6th century BC under Solon, an Athenian merchant and poet who was appointed to reform the constitution. He cancelled all debts for which land or liberty could be forfeited and established a new council (vouli) of 400 members to formulate proposals discussed in the full assembly of adult male citizens.

The tyrant Peisistratos took power in the middle of the 6th century BC, and under his rule, commerce and the arts flourished. Attica's wine and olive oil were shipped to Italy, Egypt and Asia Minor in beautiful black-figure pots; the first tragedies ever written were performed at the annual festival of the wine god, Dionysos; and the standard version of Homer's works was set down.

Further highly significant constitutional and electoral reforms were made in 508BC under Kleisthenes who created 10 artificial tribes, each based on domicile rather than blood-ties and consisting of the same number of people from the city, coast and inland. These provided military support, elected officials, and sent representatives to a new council of 500 members, which replaced Solon's 400-member council.

The Owl, symbol of Athens, on an ancient Attic Drachma coin

Persian Wars

In the 5th century BC, the Athenian army defeated the forces of the great Persian Empire to the east. In 490BC they defeated a Persian force sent by Darius I on the plain of Marathon, just 43km (26 miles) northeast of Athens. According to legend, the soldier who ran from Marathon to Athens died of exhaustion immediately after reporting

The Ancient Greek Pantheon

Following an Athens court ruling of May 2006, it is no longer illegal to worship the ancient Greek gods in Greece – and there are a surprising number of adherents of pagan ways in the country, who feel that the Judeo-Christian tradition has done untold harm to Greek society.

Here's a summary of the main deities of Mt Olympus, their legendary abode. **Zeus** rules gods and mortals, and controls the weather; his symbols are the eagle, thunder and the oak tree. **Hera** is Zeus' third and oft-betrayed wife, patroness of marriage and motherhood. **Athena**, daughter of Zeus, is goddess of wisdom and crafts, guardian of war heroes, and supposed inventor of the loom and potter's wheel. **Apollo**, a son of Zeus, is the deity of music, healing, prophecy and the sun; his advice was sought at the Delphic oracle. **Artemis** is Apollo's twin sister, goddess of hunting and the moon, and guardian of animals and young virgins. **Hermes**, another son of Zeus, was the messenger of the gods, escorter of dead souls and god of commerce, orators and writers, as well as protector of flocks, thieves and travellers. **Ares**, god of war, is yet another son of Zeus, but was unpopular on Olympus and understandably feared by mortals. Lame **Hephaestos**, god of fire, and metallurgy, still another sibling of Apollo and Ares, was the divine blacksmith, furnishing Zeus with his thunderbolts. He was married to (and frequently cuckolded by) **Aphrodite**, goddess of love, beauty and gardens. **Poseidon**, brother of Zeus, presided over seas, rivers and all creatures therein, causing storms and earthquakes with his trident; horses were also sacred to him. **Hades**, another brother of Zeus, ruled the kingdom of the dead – but also controlled all mineral wealth beneath the earth. **Demeter**, sister of Zeus, is the goddess of agriculture and protectress of crops, having bestowed corn, grain and the plough on mankind. Other revered deities include **Dionysos**, Zeus' son by a mortal, god of wine, ecstasy and the theatre; **Asklepios**, Apollo's son by a mortal, god of healing; **Themis**, goddess of justice and equity; and **Hestia**, Zeus' sister, patroness of the hearth, home and family.

The Poseidon of Artemision

the victory. His feat is commemorated in the 26-mile Olympic marathon.

Ten years later Darius I's son and successor, Xerxes, occupied Athens and burned the Acropolis, only to see his own fleet destroyed off the island of Salamis 5km (3 miles) from Piraeus.

Peloponnesian War

Following the Persian Wars, Athens and Sparta were the two most powerful Greek city-states. Each sought dominance, until their rivalry erupted in the long Peloponnesian War (431–404BC), which ended in Athenian defeat. The repressive government installed by the Spartans in Athens was overthrown by a revolt, and the Athenians allied themselves with Persia to defeat the Spartan navy in 394BC. In 338BC Athens and Thebes, now allied against the common threat of Macedonia under Philip II, were defeated at Chaironeia in Boeotia, northwest of Attica. Philip became the ruler of mainland Greece until his assassination, when he was succeeded by his son Alexander (the Great). Their rule of Athens was benign, and despite strong resentment of Macedonian domination, the city flourished.

Classical Period

The 157 years between the victory over the Persians at Salamis in 480BC and the death of Alexander the Great in 323BC were years of extraordinary intellectual and cultural activity, which became known as the Classical Period.

The great philosophers Socrates, Plato and Aristotle lived during this time, as did the playwrights Aristophanes and

Sophocles, the historians Herodotos and Thucydides, the sculptors Phidias and Praxiteles, and the statesman Pericles. The work these and many other gifted men achieved during this period laid the groundwork for much of European civilisation. Many of the physical remains of this extraordinary flowering are concentrated on the Acropolis and in the centre of the ancient city, the Greek Agora.

The Romans patronised the city after taking control of Greece in 146BC, coming to the city to study. Julius Caesar had the Roman Agora built just east of the Athenian Agora, and Hadrian (AD117–138) commissioned the construction of the Library of Hadrian and the Pantheon. In the 3rd century AD the Heruli, a Germanic tribe expelled from Scandinavia by the Danes, appeared in the Black Sea and continued south to wreak havoc in Greece. They sacked and burned Athens in AD267 before moving on to sack Corinth, Sparta and Argos.

The 5th-century BC temple of Hephaisteion in the Greek Agora

Mosaic in the Byzantine Museum

Byzantine Empire

When the Roman emperor Constantine designated Byzantium (ie Constantinople – present-day Istanbul) as his new capital in AD324, the Empire became divided into eastern and western sectors. Rome was to fall to successive waves of invaders, but Constantinople grew to thrive as the capital of the Byzantine Empire. Athens continued to serve as the great educational and cultural centre for the first two centuries of the Byzantine period. In 529, however, the Christian emperor Justinian I ordered that all the philosophical schools in Athens – which were, after all, pagan – be closed. The Parthenon and other temples elsewhere had already been turned into churches. But the closure of the schools led to the city's decline into an unimportant provincial town.

In 1204 the Fourth Crusade sacked Christian Byzantium, and Athens' fortunes were tossed among Frankish, Catalan and Italian overlords.

Ottoman Occupation

Byzantium fell in 1453 to Mehmet II and the Ottoman Turks, who reached Athens three years later. Many Albanians, who had served as mercenary troops for both the Byzantines and the Ottomans, moved to Athens and settled in Pláka.

The Turks made the Acropolis a Muslim precinct and the city acquired four large mosques, one of which is the Fethiye Mosque, still standing in the Roman Agora, as well as three hamams (baths). The Ottomans also transformed a number of churches into mosques, including the Parthenon on the Acropolis, to which they added a minaret.

The Ottoman occupation of Athens was interrupted by war with the Venetians in 1687. Besieged on the Acropolis, the Turks used the Parthenon for storing munitions. The Venetian commander, Count Morosini, brought his artillery, manned by Swedish mercenaries, to the nearby Filopáppos Hill. One shell scored a direct hit on the powder magazine, and the resulting explosion was devastating. Many Turks were killed, the Acropolis village was set on fire and the Parthenon suffered major damage for the first time.

The Turks abandoned Athens and the Venetians took over the city until a severe outbreak of plague forced them to leave after just five months. The Athenians, who had welcomed the Christian Venetians, feared retribution from the returning Ottomans and abandoned the city, leaving it uninhabited for three years. During the second period of Ottoman occupation, Pláka became the city's central commercial area. The Islamic academy, of which only the gate facing the Tower of the Winds remains, was built in 1721. The Tzisdaraki Mosque in Monastiráki Square was built in 1759.

Athenian houses under the Turkish occupation were normally built with a courtyard and, for both privacy and protection, they had few or no windows opening onto the narrow, haphazard streets. Most were two storeys high with the kitchen and storerooms on the ground floor; a wooden verandah, bedrooms, and the family common room were on the upper floor. Usually there were two knockers on the front door: one for servants and peasants; and another fancier one higher up for members of the family and upper-class visitors.

Fight for Independence

The Greek War of Independence began in the Peloponnese in 1821, and the Athenians expelled the Turks from the city the following June. Ottoman forces returned in 1826 to besiege the city, and in June 1827 they captured the Acropolis. The Greeks were obliged to sign a treaty turning Athens over to the Turks, after which the Athenians retired to the Argo-Saronic islands. The real issue was decided a few months later when, on 20 October 1827, a combined British, French and Russian fleet defeated the Turco-Egyptian fleet at Navarino on the west coast of the Peloponnese.

In 1830 the London Protocol was signed by Britain, France, Russia and Turkey recognising Greece as an independent kingdom. Otho of Bavaria was made King of Greece in 1832, and the last Turkish troops on the Acropolis surrendered in March 1833. In September 1834 Athens was officially declared the capital of Greece.

At the time, the city was little more than a village, with a population of 4,000. During the Classical Period the population had been 36,000. Several grandiose plans were submitted, including one to build a large palace on the Acropolis. Instead Sýntagma (Constitution) Square was chosen as the site for the royal palace, now the Parliament Building. The overall city plan was based on wide streets and squares within a triangle of three main streets, Ermoú, Pireós and Stadíou. Ermoú runs from Sýntagma Square to the Kerameikos archaeological site; Pireós runs from Omónia Square past the Kerameikos archaeological site to the port of Piraeus; and Stadíou runs from Omónia Square to Sýntagma Square. This triangle still defines the heart of old Athens.

Ironically, the strong German influence upon the designs of the buildings erected in post-independence Athens meant that the revival of Classical architecture in Greece was not based directly on examples of Classical antiquity, but on the neoclassical style popular in Western Europe. The University of Athens on Panepistemiou Street, by the Danish architect Christian Hansen, is a fine example of this imported neoclassical style, and there are many mansions in this genre scattered throughout Pláka and along Vasilíssis Sofías Avenue. Hansen's brother, Theophil, designed the Academy and Library.

In 1862 King Otho was deposed and replaced by a young prince from the Danish house of Glücksberg, who became George I. This royal family stayed in turbulent power until the junta arrived in 1967.

Neoclassical façade of the Academy, built between 1859–87

The 1896 Olympic Games

Early 20th Century

Within just three years of becoming Greece's capital, the population of Athens had increased almost fourfold, and steady growth continued thereafter. A particularly large wave of immigration occurred in 1922–3, the result of the exchange of populations after Greece's poorly planned advance into western Turkey was routed by resurgent Turkish nationalism under Kemal Atatürk. Approximately 390,000 Muslims moved from Greece to Turkey and 1,400,000 Greeks moved from western Turkey and eastern Thrace to Greece. Many of these Orthodox Christian refugees settled around Athens in what have now become flourishing suburbs, nostalgically named after their abandoned homes: Néa Iónia, Néa Smýrni, Néa Filadélfia (*néa* meaning new).

Between 1936 and 1941 Greece was under the military dictatorship of Ioannis Metaxas, who rejected Mussolini's demand that Greece give safe passage to the Italian army. During the winter of 1940–41 the army stopped the Italian advance into Greece, an heroic accomplishment commemorated each year with a national holiday on 28 October.

In April 1941, Germany invaded Greece defeating all Allied forces by early June, and the country was divided into Bulgarian, German and Italian occupation zones. Many Athenians starved during the following winter as all food was requisitioned. The Greek resistance movement, well established by mid-1942, became so politically divided that guerrilla fighters expended almost as much energy fighting each other as they did fighting the Germans. In October 1944, the Allied forces moved into Athens, encountering no opposition from the retreating Germans.

The war left Greece utterly devastated. Communist and royalist partisans moved steadily towards a military confrontation as the United States, under the Truman Doctrine, supported the central government. Three years of savage civil war ended in late 1949 with communist defeat. Political instability and repression persisted through the 1950s.

Reign of the Colonels

On 21 April 1967, the military seized power and tanks rolled on to the streets of Athens. During the seven-year dictatorship of the 'colonels' junta' under George Papadopoulos, political parties were dissolved, the press was censored and left-wing sympathisers were exiled, tortured and imprisoned. In December 1967, King Constantine led an ineffective counter-coup and was obliged to leave the country. In June 1973 Greece was declared a republic, with Papadopoulos as its first president.

Andiparohí

One of the first post-World War II parliaments introduced *andiparohí*, which drastically changed the appearance of a city that had grown organically since the 1830s. Under this law, the owners of a refugee shack or crumbling neoclassical mansion could turn over their property to a developer, who would knock it down and erect a block of flats, allotting two or three to the provider of the site in exchange. Both benefited: the developer didn't have to buy land, and the donating family received free real estate. But Athens suffered aesthetically as dreary concrete buildings spread everywhere between the 1950s and 1970s, leaving little green space or many buildings of distinction.

On 17 November of the same year a major student protest at Athens Polytechnic was brutally crushed by armoured vehicles, leaving dozens killed. The end came eight months later when the junta attempted to overthrow the Cypriot president, Archbishop Makários, provoking the Turkish invasion of Cyprus. The junta's attempt to defend Cyprus was so inept that senior military commanders overthrew the junta. Constantine Karamanlís, the former conservative premier, was recalled from exile in Paris to restore democracy. The reforms that followed included a referendum that abolished the monarchy.

The Way Forward

With its entry into the EC in 1981, Greece's economic prospects strengthened. That same year, the first socialist government swept to victory under charismatic Andreas Papandreou and the PASOK party. Papandreou presented a centre-leftist front, recognising the communist and leftist resistance organisations who had fought against the German occupation. In the long run, this was a major contribution to political stability, as was the 1989 destruction of all secret police files. In early 2004, the country again came under the

A National Guard *(évzonos)*

rule of the New Democracy party, led by Kostas Karamanlís, nephew of the party's founder. The dynastic tradition continues with PASOK now led by George Papandreou, the son of Andreas. Karamanlís narrowly won a second term in September 2007. But whatever the family or party, Greece is a stable, modern democracy with a growing economy.

Historical Landmarks

1150–750BC The Dark Age.

750–480BC The Archaic Period.

594/3BC Solon breaks aristocratic power.

508BC Kleisthenes introduces democracy in Athens.

490BC First Persian War. Greeks win at Marathon.

480–323BC The Classical Period.

480BC Athenian fleet defeats Persians in the Strait of Salamis.

477BC Athens unites allies under the League of Delos.

459–429BC The Golden Age of Pericles.

447–432BC The Parthenon is built on the Acropolis.

431–404BC Peloponnesian War; Sparta defeats Athens.

338BC Philip II of Macedon acquires Athens.

336–323BC Alexander the Great rules Greece.

323–146BC The Hellenistic Period.

146BC–AD330 Roman rule.

AD49/50 St Paul brings Christianity to Athens.

AD529 From Byzantium, Emperor Justinian orders closure of all philosophy schools; Athens goes into decline.

1456 Athens falls to the Ottoman Turks.

1687 Venetians besiege Athens; Parthenon blown up. The city is abandoned for three years.

1759 Tzidaraki Mosque built in Monastiráki Square.

1821–33 Greek War of Independence.

1834 Athens becomes the capital of Greece.

1923 Greeks from Asia Minor flood into Athens.

1941–4 Axis powers occupy Greece.

1946–9 Greek Civil War ends with Communist defeat.

1951 Greece becomes a member of nato.

1967–74 Military junta rules Greece.

1981 Greece joins the EC.

2002 The euro replaces the drachma.

2004 Athens hosts Olympic Games.

WHERE TO GO

Viewed from the air – or from the heights of the Acropolis or Mount Lykavittós – Athens is a sprawling city: a maze of apartment blocks and office buildings stretching to the horizon. Yet central Athens is remarkably compact. Most major sites are within walking distance of one another, while the metro and trolley-bus systems provide an inexpensive, reliable means of transport for those who become footsore.

Ancient remains are scattered across the central area. Athens has grown incrementally throughout its history, resulting in numerous districts, each with its own particular character. This guide divides the city into a number of sections, covering the ancient centre of the city first and then moving out in a clockwise spiral through the other important neighbourhoods.

Ancient Athens was centred around the Acropolis, with sacred temples built atop the rock and the city spread out below. Today the area is still replete with Greek and Roman remains, though these are interspersed with later buildings – a fascinating mixture of neoclassical mansions and terraced cottages dating back to Ottoman times. This area, known as Pláka, is one of the most charming parts of Athens, attracting visitors from every corner of the world.

THE ACROPOLIS

It's impossible to overestimate the importance of the **Acropolis** (daily Apr–Oct 8am–7.30pm, Nov–Mar 8am–5pm; charge) to the ancient Greeks. The religious significance of this sheer-sided rock, looming 90m (300ft) above the town,

View of the Acropolis from the southwest

Remains of sculptures on the east pediment of the Parthenon

was paramount, and the buildings on the summit still embody the essence of classical Greek architecture. You can see these temples from most parts of the city – particularly at night when they are beautifully lit – which adds to the feeling that this small area is still the heart of the city. The name 'Acropolis' derives from the Greek words *ákro* meaning 'highest point' and *pólis*, meaning town.

Try to visit early or late in the day to avoid the tour groups, or on Mondays, when most tours don't operate; and remember to wear comfortable rubber-soled shoes as there are slippery stones worn smooth over the centuries and numerous uneven areas where heels can catch.

Once past the ticket office a path leads to the summit of the Acropolis – a relatively flat plateau around 320m by 130m (1,050ft by 425ft) in area. This steep incline is the last section of the original route taken by the Panathenaic procession up to the statue of Athena *(see box, page 49)*.

Used for strategic purposes throughout the Mycenaean and Archaic periods, the rock was easy to defend; it had a water supply and superb views of the surrounding area. The first religious structures appeared at the end of the 6th century BC, though these early temples were destroyed by the Persian forces of Xerxes in 480BC. The Athenians left the gutted temples untouched for 30 years and were only persuaded by Pericles to undertake a reconstruction programme in 450BC.

Pericles commissioned the Parthenon, the Erechtheion, the Temple of Athena Nike (currently being reconstructed) and the Propylaia, taking advantage of a new marble quarry on Mount Pendéli (Pentele to the ancients); and the marble became known as Pentelic. When the Romans took control of Athens they embellished the site with small additions, but the decline of Roman power left the Acropolis vulnerable to attack and vandalism. The rock reverted to its earliest use as a strategic stronghold during Ottoman rule. Large quantities of stone from the temples were used for construction of bastions and domestic buildings.

Following Greek independence in the 19th century, a zealous restoration project saw the removal of all medieval and Ottoman structures on the Acropolis, and harkened the beginning of archaeological studies of the ancient remains. These continue to the present day.

The Propylaia

As you make your way up towards the Propylaia (gateway) you will pass through the **Beule Gate**, built as part of a 3rd-century AD defensive wall. This gate was unearthed only in the 19th century from tons of rubble from the Acropolis. More like a temple than a gateway, the monumental **Propylaia** was a sign of things to come, built to impress and inspire visitors. It retains this ability in modern times, even though the structure was never actually completed.

Construction commenced in 437BC to a plan by the brilliant Athenian architect, Mnisikles. A series of six Doric columns marks the transition into the **Propylaia**, beyond which there are four symmetrical rooms, two on either side of the walkway. Two rows of three Ionic columns (this was the first building to incorporate both styles of column) support the roof, whose coffered ceiling was originally painted as a heavenly scene. The five heavy wooden doors along the walkway would have heightened the tension of those ancient

A Greek Who's Who

As the cradle of democracy, history, philosophy, drama and comedy, it's not surprising that Athens was the birthplace of the most illustrious figures in ancient history. Here are just a few:

Socrates (c. 469–399BC): philosopher and orator who pursued truth through dialectic discourse.

Plato (c. 428–347BC): student of Socrates, political and religious philosopher; founded his own academy of higher study.

Aristotle (384–322BC): philosopher; student at Plato's academy and tutor to Alexander the Great.

Herodotus (484–425BC): 'Father of history'; wrote thorough accounts of the early Persian wars and dynastic struggles in Asia Minor.

Thucydides (c. 460–400BC): chronicled the Peloponnesian Wars with the first analytical methodology for recording history.

Pericles (c. 495–429BC): Athenian statesman during the city's Golden Age; responsible for construction of the Parthenon.

Kallikrates and **Iktinos**: architects of the Parthenon (447–432BC).

Pheidias (c. 490–430BC) and **Praxiteles**: sculptors.

Aeschylus (525–456BC), **Sophocles** (497–406BC) and **Euripides** (480–406BC): great tragic dramatists; Euripides in particular wrote plays about ordinary mortals rather than mortals interacting with gods.

Aristophanes (448–385BC): originator of Greek comedy.

pilgrims, as each would be opened in turn. The only room to have been completed was the second on the northern side. This was used as a rest room for visitors to the Acropolis and also, according to the 2nd-century AD Greek traveller Pausanias, as a picture gallery *(Pinakothíki)*, since its walls were covered with panels and frescoes.

The Propylaia seen from below

Having made your way through the Propylaia, if you can be deterred from going directly to the immense structure of the Parthenon, on your right you may find the remains of the **Sanctuary of Artemis Brauronia**, founded in the 4th century BC.

The Parthenon

The **Parthenon** is one of the most recognisable buildings in the world. The series of columns supporting pediment and frieze is the epitome of Athens to many visitors, and would also have been to travellers in ancient times. However, they would have seen a structure with a veneer of splendid colour and decorated with magnificently carved sculptures, not to mention a strong wooden roof. What remains is the bare Pentelic marble used in the construction, and the refined lines and form that make it an architectural masterpiece.

The Parthenon was dedicated to Athena, goddess of wisdom and justice, and means Temple of the Virgin. It also housed the city's treasury, bringing together spiritual and secular powers. An Archaic temple on the site was removed after the battle of Marathon in 490BC to make room for a much larger temple. This so-called older Parthenon was still being constructed when the Persians destroyed the Acropolis temples in 480BC. Work on the present temple, designed by Kallikrates and Iktinos and led by Pericles, began in 447BC. The temple was dedicated to Athena in 438BC, at the Panathenaic Festival. This festival then took place every four years until the late 4th century AD *(see box, page 49)*.

The Parthenon was converted into a church in the 6th century, and a bell tower was added by the Byzantines who named it Agía Sofía, meaning the Holy Wisdom. During the 15th century, under Ottoman rule, the bell tower became a minaret and the church was converted into a mosque.

Eventually the building was put to use as a powder magazine. In September 1687, when Venetian forces attacked Athens, a shell hit the Parthenon, igniting the powder inside.

The ruins of the Parthenon at the summit of the Acropolis

The resulting explosion destroyed the centre of the temple along with many priceless carved friezes and columns. Under a 'licence' from the sultan, Lord Elgin arranged to remove as much of the Parthenon's sculpture as his men could cut free, a process that continued from 1801 until 1811. The items, known as the **Elgin Marbles**, are on display in the British Museum, though the legiti-

Optical illusion

There are no straight lines anywhere in the Parthenon; the ancient designers deliberately used a technique known as *entasis*, with gradual curves in lintels or pediments, and columns with bulging centres. This sophisticated optical illusion leaves the impression that the building is in fact completely squared on the vertical and horizontal.

macy of holding on to them is hotly disputed. Restoration on what remains of the temple has been almost constant since 1834.

Today it is not possible to walk among the columns and what remains of the inner temple. This echoes the rules of ancient Greece, when only the highest priests could enter the *naos* or central sanctuary. There they would have been able to worship an ivory-and-gold-covered wooden statue of Athena said to have been 12m (39ft) high. Walk around the 70m-by-30m (230ft-by-100ft) exterior to appreciate the grace of the columns.

The Erechtheion and Porch of the Caryatids

To the north of the Parthenon stand the graceful statues of the **Porch of the Caryatids**, which adorn the southern façade of the **Erechtheion**. This temple is an unusual mélange of styles, with rooms at varying levels, where the worship of three gods took place. It was the last of Pericles' great buildings to be finished, dedicated in 406BC. Built beside an ancient Temple of Athena whose scant remains can just be seen, the Erechtheion

The Porch of the Caryatids

brought together the worship of Athena and Poseidon under one roof. Legend says that following the contest between the two gods for the honour of protecting Athens, they were reconciled and this dual temple recognised their special bond with regard to the city. The sanctuary was converted into a church in the 6th century AD and was used to house the governor's harem during Ottoman times.

The **caryatids** – female figures used as pillars – are so named because they were long presumed to be depictions of the women from Peloponnesian Caryae, captured after that city-state made an alliance with the Persians and was sacked in punishment. Now, however, it is thought more likely that they represent temple novices in the service of the goddess Athena. The sculptures are copies: four of the originals are displayed in the Acropolis Museum; one is in the British Museum; the sixth was lost during the Ottoman period. On the eastern façade a row of Ionic columns marks the entrance to the sanctuary of Athena Polias, established here after the Old Temple of Athena was destroyed by the Persians in 480BC. The foundations of the Old Temple of Athena are in a roped-off area directly south of the Erechtheion.

A large north porch balances that of the southern Porch of the Caryatids. This sits on high foundations as the ground level drops on the northern side. A hole in the ceiling and a gap in the floor were left to show where Poseidon struck with his trident. In great antiquity the Greeks believed that a god in the form of a snake lived within the Acropolis. The half-man, half-god Erechtheos, a later personification of this deity, was believed to have been buried beneath the sanctuary; worshippers dropped him food through the gap in the floor. Outside the porch to the west there was an altar to Zeus, of which nothing remains. The altar was said to be beneath the olive tree Athena gave to the city.

Views from the Acropolis

When you've finished exploring the Acropolis, take time to enjoy the views from its walls. Sections of the stone defences date back to the Mycenaean era. From the northeast corner, by the flag pole, you can see several of the other major archaeological sites and the district of Pláka below. The wooded slopes of Mount Lykavittós, with the smart area of Kolonáki on its lower slopes, is to the northeast. The coast and the islands of the Saronic Gulf lie to the southwest.

The old Acropolis Museum, which stands at the far, eastern end of the site, had its collection transferred to the New Acropolis Museum *(see page 37)* in 2007/8. It is now used for temporary exhibitions.

AROUND THE ACROPOLIS

A number of other archaeological remains – including the Odeion of Herodes Atticus, the Theatre of Dionysos, the Monument of Filopáppos, the Hill of the Pnyx and the Hill of Areopagus – can be found on the flanks of the Acropolis and on nearby hills. Head south of the rock by turning left out of the main entrance and you will reach the first after a five-minute walk.

The Odeion of Herodes Atticus

The Odeion of Herodes Atticus (Iródio)

The **Odeion of Herodes Atticus** (known as the Iródio in Greek) was built in AD161–174 in Roman style with a three-storey stage and an auditorium capable of seating 5,000 spectators. It was destroyed during the 3rd century AD and in the 18th century the Ottomans used material from the ruins to build a defensive wall. In the 1950s it was restored and now provides the venue for spectacular outdoor summer performances held by the **Hellenic Festival** *(see page 82)*.

The Theatre of Dionysos

Set into the hillside on the southeastern flank of the Acropolis are the extensive remains of the **Theatre of Dionysos** (daily May–Oct 8am–7.30pm, Nov–Apr 8am–5pm; charge or included in Acropolis ticket), built in the 5th century BC and upgraded two centuries later. In Roman times a long colonnaded stoa and promenade linked it with the Odeion of Herodes Atticus, of which little remains. The theatre was the birthplace of dramatic and comic art and formed the social and political heart of Athens during its 'golden age'. The premieres of several major pieces by Sophocles, Euripides and Aristophanes were performed here, and the Athenian assembly also met here late in its history. The auditorium originally held 15,000. Most interesting are the carved front-row thrones for VIPs, including one with lion's-claw feet reserved for the high priest of Dionysos. The so-called **Stage of Phaedrus** depicting scenes from the life of Dionysos dates from the 4th century AD. Surrounding the theatre are remains of several other buildings including an **Asklepeion** (shrine of healing) and the **Odeion of Pericles**.

New Acropolis Museum

Opposite the old theatre stands the shining modern construction of the **New Acropolis Museum**, the latest addition to the Athens cultural scene. At the time of writing there was no information on likely opening hours or admission prices, but the building was expected to be open to the public from early 2009.

There was no doubt that it would be a stunning museum, with its angular design by the architect Bernard Tschumi and building cost of €130 million. The Greeks hope that one day the top floor will showcase what they call the Parthenon Marbles and what most other people refer to as the Elgin Marbles *(see page 33)*. They will be housed in a vast glass gallery, aligned as

Entrance to the
New Acropolis Museum

they would have been when they were on the Parthenon, and with the Parthenon itself an impressive sight through the glass walls. Meanwhile, other floors contain the Acropolis antiquities – mostly marble sculptures dating to the 6th and 5th centuries BC – as well as displays on how the Acropolis was first settled, and how the Parthenon and its other buildings were constructed.

In constructing the new museum, parts of the old city of Athens were discovered on the site. This was one reason for the delay in the opening: the building's plans had to be altered so that the remains of the old city will be left where they stood, but visible to visitors through glass floors laid to protect the precious items. The New Acropolis Museum is expected to become an essential part of an Athens visit.

The Monument of Filopáppos

Filopáppos Monument

Southwest of the Acropolis stands the **Monument of Filopáppos**, built in AD116 as a grave for the last titular ruler of Commagene. This small Hellenic kingdom located in modern southeastern Turkey was independent from 162BC until AD72. When Filopáppos lived in Athens as a Roman consul there was no longer a Commagene to rule but he was generous to his adopted city, which responded with this impressive funeral monument. The convex façade has a sculptured frieze depicting Filopáppos riding a chariot and performing his duties in the senate. The view of the Acropolis from here is incomparable; the easiest way up is by paved path from the brilliantly frescoed Byzantine church of **Ágios Dimítrios Loumbardiáris**.

The Hill of the Pnyx

North of Ágios Dimítrios Loumbardiáris rises the **Hill of the Pnyx**, meeting place of the Assembly of Athens. Loosely translated, *pnyx* means 'crowded or tightly packed place', and in ancient times this was a highly populated area. You'll see the outlines of walls, including the defensive **Themistoklean Wall**, between the bushes or under the turf as you walk. The Pnyx meeting place can be found below the summit on the northeastern side of the hill. When democracy was established at the end of the 6th century BC, the debating chamber moved from the Agora to this structure, where the great Greek statesmen made their speeches at the rostrum. Seats were provided for the 5,000 citizens of the city needed for a decision-making quorum, who would listen to the arguments of Pericles and Themistocles. On the **Hill of the Nymphs** north of the Pnyx you'll see the neoclassical lines of the original **Athens Observatory**, founded in 1842.

The Hill of Areopagus

On the north flank of the Acropolis is the **Hill of Areopagus**, diagonally down to the north of the main Acropolis ticket office. This was the meeting place for the governing council in aristocratic periods, and remained the court of criminal justice even in the democratic era; the modern Greek supreme court is still called the *Áreos Págos* (Hill of Mars). Here in AD51 St Paul delivered his speech known as the *Sermon on the Unknown God*. A bronze plaque with the sermon in Greek is to the right of the slippery steps leading to the top.

PLÁKA AND ANAFIÓTIKA

After exploring these fascinating sites, you'll be ready for a rest and change of scenery. As you make your way towards the modern city you'll pass through two small districts that offer a range of cafés, bars and tavernas, along with images of Greek daily life not found in more modern parts of Athens.

Anafiótika hugs the high ground immediately below the Acropolis, and can be reached semi-directly from the Areopagus. Built during the 19th century by people from the small Cycladic island of Anáfi, today the narrow lanes with their neat, whitewashed cottages and plethora of potted geraniums are still reminiscent of their Aegean roots.

Pláka lies below Anafiótika and fills the space between the ancient and modern city, extending almost to Mitropóleos and Filellínon streets. This was the centre of population from

The pedestrianised area of Pláka at the heart of old Athens

Byzantine times through to Greek independence. The maze of narrow, mostly pedestrianised thoroughfares is a delight to explore with its many neoclassical mansions and humbler houses, and there are numerous shops and eateries to choose from. You may be lucky to hear a *laterna* as it's wheeled by its keeper through the streets; these hand-turned

Museum of Greek Folk Art

barrel organs playing *rebétika* tunes are now becoming extremely rare, and donations are much appreciated.

Pláka is particularly atmospheric in the evenings when locals enjoy a *volta,* or stroll, before dinner and tavernas set tables out on the narrower lanes. These open out onto quiet squares often dominated by Byzantine churches or older monuments; the neoclassical buildings are now strictly protected, and this is the one part of the city which, superficially at least, gives a taste of what Athens before 1900 was like.

Pláka Museums

At Kydathinéon 17, the **Museum of Greek Folk Art** (Tue–Sun 9am–2pm; charge) offers an interesting collection of embroidery, lace and liturgical garments, as well as a wonderful display of paintings by the early 20th-century folk artist Theofilos. Spinning and weaving are also highlighted, along with traditional puppets, festival masks and costumes. Nearby at Kydathinéon 14, the **Children's Museum** (Tue–Fri 10am–2pm, Sat–Sun 10am–3pm, closed July–Aug; tel: 210 331 2995; free) has plenty of hands-on activities for youngsters.

At the southern end of Odós Adrianoú, in a small square surrounded by cafés, stands the **Monument of Lysikratos**. Dating from the 4th century BC, it consists of a series of curved panels and columns creating a circular structure supporting a dome made from a single block of Pentelic marble. Originally, this was topped by a bronze tripod – a prize awarded in choral competitions during the Classical era. During the 18th century a Capuchin monastery occupied the land all around the monument and the interior of the base was used as a guest room. Lord Byron stayed here in 1810.

High up near the Acropolis, the **Kanellopoulos Museum** (closed for restoration) occupies a mansion on Odós Panós. Opened in 1976, and recently refitted, the building contains an eclectic family collection of artefacts, including Geometric-to-Hellenistic-period artwork, Roman funerary ornaments from Fayum, and Byzantine icons, jewellery, frescoes and tapestries.

Athens' Cathedral

The Greek and Roman agoras delimit the western end of Pláka. To reach them from the southeastern area of Pláka, walk along Odós Adrianoú. A short diversion northeast along Paleológou takes you to Athens' cathedral, the **Mitrópolis**. With ground broken in 1842 after Greek independence, it was completed in 1862, financed by the sale of land and structures pertaining to 72 churches; marble from these churches was used in the cathedral walls. The cathedral houses the relics of Agía Filothéi, who was martyred by the Ottomans in 1589 (and who appeared in a vision to the faithful in 1940, foretelling Greece's ordeal during the occupation but victorious emergence thereafter). To the left of the entrance is also the marble sarcophagus of Patriarch Grigorios (Gregory) V, who was executed by the Turks in Istanbul, when the Greek war of independence erupted in 1821, and whose corpse (after numerous adventures) only arrived here in 1871.

In the shadow of the main cathedral huddles the tiny **Mikrí Mitrópolis** (Little Cathedral), doubly dedicated to the Panagía Gorgoepikoös (She Who is Quick to Hear) and Ágios Eleuthérios, protector of women in childbirth. Dating from the 12th century, the church was built using stone from the ancient sites of the city. Wander around its exterior walls to see sections of Greek and Roman columns, or fragments of ornate bas-reliefs. Nearby – where Mitropóleos meets Pendélis – is another church, **Agía Dynámis**,

Outside the Mitrópolis

meaning 'Divine Strength'. This tiny place of worship has survived the redevelopment of the district, but now sits right underneath the modern Ministry of Religion and Education.

The Roman Agora

Where Adrianoú intersects Eólou, turn south on the latter to reach the **Roman Agora** (daily Apr–Oct 8am–7.30pm, Nov–Mar 8am–5pm; charge or included in Acropolis ticket), first established during the 2nd century BC to accommodate an expanding Athens. The ornate entrance gate was commissioned by Julius Caesar in honour of Athena in her avatar of Archegetis (Commander of the City). Much of the north and west wall of the Agora lies unexcavated under the houses of

Pláka, but the south wall and the remains of the south colonnade are there, along with a series of shops. The most remarkable building in the complex (though it was outside the Agora when built) is the **Tower of the Winds**. This octagonal structure was a *klepsydra* or water-clock built by a Greek from Syria, Andronikos Kyrristos, in the 1st century BC. Each of the eight faces is decorated with a beautiful frieze depicting a personification of the wind blowing from that direction. The timing device was water-driven with a supply from the Acropolis above.

Just west of the Tower of the Winds you'll see one of only two mosques still standing in the city, the **Fethiye Tzami**.

Ottoman Athens

Until recently locals have not been keen to highlight monuments erected by the Ottoman conquerors, but it was the juxtaposition of the elements of an oriental bazaar with remains of the more distant past that most intrigued the first Grand Tourists who showed up in Athens late in the 18th century. The Ottomans did not consider Athens an especially important town, and so far as we know endowed it with just three purpose-built mosques (not counting churches converted for Islamic worship). These were the Fethiye and Tzidarakis mosques, and the Küçuk Tzami, just south of the Roman agora, though only foundations of the latter remain. There were also several *hamams* or baths, though the only survivor is the intriguing Abdi Efendi baths at Kirrýstou 8 (Wed–Mon 9am–2.30pm; charge), built in phases from the 15th to the 17th centuries. Nearby, opposite the Tower of the Winds, stands a surviving gateway of an 18th-century *medresse* or Koranic academy, later used as a prison and demolished around 1900. The Tower of the Winds itself (*Aérides* in Greek) was used during the Ottoman period as a lodge of a dervish order, who terrified their Orthodox neighbours with their chanting and dancing.

Built shortly after the Ottoman conquest, it now houses an archaeological storehouse and is not open to the public, though a proposal is afoot to make it available for use by the city's large contemporary Muslim population, who have no proper mosque. Nearby on Odós Diogénous is the **Museum of Greek Popular Musical Instruments** (Tue and Thur–Sun 10am–2pm, Wed noon–6pm; free), with a fascinating and well-dis-

The Tower of the Winds

played collection of instruments and musical recordings bringing the varied regional folk music of Greece to life.

The Greek Agora

From the south side of the Roman Agora, continue west along Polygnótou to the southeast entrance of the **ancient Greek Agora** (daily May–Oct 8am–7.30pm, Nov–Apr 8am–4.30pm; charge or included in Acropolis ticket), birthplace of western democracy and the social, commercial and administrative heart of the ancient city-state of Athens (*agora* is derived from the Greek *agiero*, meaning to assemble). From the 6th century BC onwards, this area played host to a number of activities including religious and political meetings, law courts, education, shopping or simply passing the time of day. Here Socrates presented his philosophical theories; unfortunately for him he fell foul of the authorities and was put to death in 403BC. The area was mostly razed during the Goth attacks of AD267, but was covered with new buildings during Byzantine and Ottoman times, all of which had to be cleared when excavations began.

From the southeastern entrance, follow a section of the Panathenaic Way past the 11th-century church of **Ágii Após-toli**, the only remaining Byzantine building on the site. Greatly changed over the centuries, it was restored to its original form in the late 1950s. The paintings in the narthex are original; others were moved from the Hephaisteion when it was deconsecrated. The Panathenaic Way continues to the other entrance off Adrianoú, near which can be seen the one corner remaining of the **Altar of the Twelve Gods**, a small monument from where distances from Athens to all other points in the Greek world were measured. Directly to its south, the outline of the **Altar of Ares** and **Temple of Ares** can be seen in gravel. Beyond them are the remains of the huge **Odeion of Agrippa**, a roofed theatre built in 15BC. Before it are three gigantic statues of a god and two tritons.

The Stoa of Attalos

The eastern side of the Agora is dominated by the **Stoa of Attalos**. First erected by King Attalos II of Pergamon and opened in 138BC, it was faithfully recreated during the 1950s, giving a stunning vision of what communal buildings were like in ancient times. Stoas were very popular in antiquity and all large settlements had at least one. These long colonnaded porches provided shade in summer and shelter in winter and were often used to link important community

One of the Odeion's tritons

The reconstructed Stoa of Attalos in the ancient Greek Agora

buildings. The Stoa of Attalos was a two-storey structure with small shops at the back. Today it houses the excavation offices and the excellent **Stoa of Attalos Museum** (hours as for site; admission included in site charge). Here you'll find a wide range of artefacts from the ancient Agora site including six bronze ballots used in the deliberations of the *parabyston* or Court of the Eleven, concerned with criminal justice. Look out too for the *ostraka*, or clay tablets, bearing the names of those banished, or 'ostracised', from Athens for ten years – Hippokrates, Themistokles and Aristeides the Just being a few of the more famous exiles.

The Hephaisteion

The western side of the Agora is dominated by the best-preserved ancient Greek temple in the world, the **Hephaisteion** (Temple of Hephaistos; also known, incorrectly, as the Theseion). The design of the temple is Doric mixed with

The 5th-century BC Temple of Hephaisteion

Ionic elements; it was completed between 449 and 444BC. Hephaistos was the god of metallurgy, and this temple was set at the heart of the smithing, casting and ironmongery district. Later it was converted into the church of Ágios Geórgios with the addition of interior walls and a vaulted roof, surviving through Ottoman times – the last services were performed in 1834. It then served as a museum and storehouse.

The exterior of the temple is well preserved and uses the same building techniques as the Parthenon, though the columns are more slender and the entablature (the space above the column capitals and below the pediments) sturdier. The metopes (square spaces, often carved in relief, between the triglyphs in a Doric frieze) on the entablature depict the legendary feats of Hercules and Theseus, the latter subject accounting for the long-standing misidentification of the temple. Surrounding the temple is a landscaped area with the same plant species used in a garden that existed here in antiquity, irrigated by a spring on the Hill of the Pnyx.

South of the Hephaisteion along the paved path is an open area with a large reconstructed **site plan** displayed in a case. This gives a clear view of the Agora together with an impression of what it looked like in AD150.

The Tholos and Bouleuterion

Following the path through the Agora you'll see the round **Tholos** or **Prytaneion**, built in 465BC as the assembly and dining hall for the *prytanes*, a governing committee responsible for the city's daily business. The 50 members of each tribal contingent took turns serving for approximately one month on this executive committee, and during this month they were fed at public expense in the Tholos. At night at least 17 senators slept here so that decisions could be made in cases of emergency. Immediately north of the Tholos is the site of the original **Bouleuterion** (Council Chamber), constructed after the reforms of Kleisthenes in 508BC; most traces of it were erased when the **Metroön** or Temple of the Mother of the Gods was erected here late in the 5th century BC, when the **New Bouleuterion** was built just to the west.

The Panathenaic Festival

This important festival was made popular by Peisistratos (ruled 546–528BC). It was held every four years in August, in honour of the goddess Athena. The festivities comprised athletic contests and musical events, and the winners were given vials containing olive oil from the fruit of the sacred groves of Athens. However, the most important element of the celebration was a procession that led from Kerameikos through the Agora along the Panathenaic Way (aka Sacred Way), finishing at the Parthenon, the temple dedicated to Athena. At the head of the procession, on a ship set on wheels and propelled by priests and priestesses, was an embroidered garment to adorn the cult statue of Athena. This had been woven by the female guardians of the temple – the *Arrhephoroi*. Once within the sacred precincts, animal sacrifices were made before the statue was robed and the procession dispersed, but doubtless festivities of some sort continued, with a carnival atmosphere prevailing across the city for some days.

MONASTIRÁKI

The area immediately northeast of the ancient Greek Agora is known as Monastiráki, one of the most colourful parts of Athens. South of Odós Ermoú, which approximately bisects the district, the mostly pedestrianised streets are full of pavement cafés, shops selling religious articles, more overtly touristic boutiques selling souvenirs such as ceramics, sandals and copper kitsch, and (centred on Platía Avyssinías) the true used-furniture-and-metalware **flea market**, which comes alive at weekends. North of Ermoú lies more practical, workaday shops, especially in the sub-district of **Psyrrí**, which is also a major nightlife hub, well colonised with tavernas, ouzeris and cafés. Ermoú itself forges east to Sýntagma Square *(see page 59)*, with high-end retail outlets along the intial stretch to either side of a little square that's home to the beautiful 11th-century Byzantine church of **Kapnikaréa**. Its octagonal dome is supported by four columns and its vivid frescoes were created in the 1950s by the Asia-Minor-born artist Fotis Kondoglou. Kapnikaréa was earmarked for demolition in the 1830s, but was saved by the personal intervention of Prince Ludwig of Bavaria, father of Greece's first king.

Monastiráki, one of the most colourful parts of the city

Monastiráki Square

The district revolves around **Monastiráki Square** (Platía Monastirakioú), always crowded with commuters hurrying to the Art Nouveau metro station, barrow-vendors of fruit and nuts, and itinerant peddlers of pirate CDs, watches and mobile phones. The originally 11th-century church at its centre – **Panagía Pandánassa** – was rebuilt in 1678 as the heart of a much larger convent, all of whose outbuildings have vanished. The south side of the square is dominated by the **Tzisdarákis Mosque**, built in 1759 by the Ottoman governor. It now houses the Greek Folk Art Museum's collection of folk pottery (Wed–Mon 9am–2.30pm; charge).

Just up Áreos from the mosque stands **Hadrian's Library**, built in AD132 around a garden-courtyard with an ornamental pool. Only the west wall and a stretch of colonnade are now standing, but after years of desultory excavations a part of the grounds are now open to the public (daily Apr–Oct 8am–7.30pm, Nov–Mar 8.30–3pm; charge).

Benaki Museum Collection of Islamic Art

When the Benaki Museum *(see page 63)* was renovated in 2000 to focus on Greek history, all the fine Islamic art objects from the collection were moved to this excellent new museum at in the Psyrrí district behind the Kerameikos archaeological site (Tue–Sun 9am–3pm, Wed until 9pm; charge).

Benaki's Islamic collection contains over 8,000 items on display across four floors of two specially converted neoclassical mansions. The objects are presented roughly chronologically, and a map in each room shows the extent of the Islamic empire at that time. There are astronomical instruments, decorated rifles and daggers, illuminated manuscripts, dazzling ceramics, and many other objects that are breathtaking in their beauty. The ornate reception room from a Cairo mansion, re-created on the third floor, is a highlight.

Kerameikos and Gázi

The most pleasant way to reach the archaeological site of **Kerameikos** (daily Apr–Oct 8am–7.30pm, Nov–Mar 8.30am–3pm; charge or joint ticket with Acropolis) on foot is not by following busy Ermoú which bounds it to the south, but by cutting through Psyrrí district, perhaps stopping for lunch at one of the ouzeris or tavernas just off its central Iróön Square. The archaeological site incorporates a section of the 478BC city wall, and the entrance gate into Athens from Eleusis to the west and Pireás to the south.

The Panathenaic Procession *(see page 49)* would start from here on its journey to the Acropolis, and the procession of the Eleusian Mysteries would leave the city from here via the Sacred Gate and along the **Sacred Way**. The most important building found here, dating in its present version from Roman times, is the **Pompeion**, where procession paraphernalia was stored and where those involved would ready themselves.

Kerameikos funerary monument

Kerameikos was named after the potters who worked here within the city walls (Inner Kerameikos), on the site of good clay deposits along the banks of the River Eridanos. Their work was transported around the Greek world, but the pots were not considered to be of any great value, designed to be used – and broken – within a year or so.

Outside the wall (Outer Kerameikos) was the major cemetery of the city (it was forbidden to bury the dead within the city walls), with burials dating from the 12th century BC. Major figures from Greek history were buried here, and their funerary monuments are some of the most exquisite items found during excavations around the city. The on-site **Oberlander Museum** exhibits burial finds dating from the 12th to 6th centuries BC, but you'll see many more in the National Archaeological Museum *(see page 54)*.

For those whose artistic tastes lean more towards post-industrial landscapes, just beyond Kerameikos – across Odós Pireós – is the old gas works of **Gázi**, with its round tank, stacks and warehouses; these have been converted into the **Technopolis**, which hosts cultural events and exhibitions.

OMÓNIA AND ENVIRONS

From Monastiráki, the parallel thoroughfares of Athinás and pedestrianised Eólou (more comfortable for walking) lead straight north to Omónia Square (Platía Omonías; Omónia means Concord), the apex of the traditional commercial triangle. Either street leads through the central market area, one of the most fascinating (and non-touristy) districts of Athens. Quieter Eólou offers, next to a little square with a flower market, the church of **Agía Iríni**, where superb chanting takes place on Sunday mornings. Near the top of its course Eólou passes Platía Kotziá (aka Platía Dimarhíou), flanked by the National Bank of Greece occupying an 1884-vintage neoclassical mansion, and the *dimarhío* (town hall) itself.

Busier Athinás forges up to Evripídou with its spice stalls and the **Varvákio**, the 1870s-built meat-and-fish market on the right; the meat section works long hours, and also hosts

Transformation

If Evripídou is the traditional spice bazaar, Sofokléous was historically home to Athens' longest-established red-light district. Since the mid-1990s, however, the prostitutes have moved to a district northwest of the Kerameikos site, and the seedy hotels along Sofokléous are slowly being upgraded – in the case of the futuristic Fresh Hotel *(see page 132)*, spectacularly so.

several restaurants serving *patsás* (tripe soup), the traditional Greek hangover cure. Fruits and vegetables are sold on Platía Varvakíou to the left, and further on, at the edge of Pysrrí, is the heart of Athens' '**Little Asia**', full of Bangladeshi, Pakistani and Chinese shops. **Omónia Square**, when you finally reach it, proves anti-climactic, a constant race-track of traffic, though it has been spruced up since the millennium.

The National Archaeological Museum

A 10-minute walk north of the square along Odós Patissíon brings you to the **National Archaeological Museum** (Mon 1–7.30pm, Tue–Sun 8am–7.30pm; charge), one of the most prestigious archaeological collections in the world. Finds cover 7,000 years of Greek history, and have been collected from numerous sites across the nation. The museum brings the ancient Greek world to life, shedding light on almost every aspect of the citizens' daily activities. Devote at least a couple of hours to this amazing display, which was over-hauled in phases from 2002 to 2005.

Directly ahead of you as you enter, the prehistoric collection (rooms 3–6) contains the treasure trove unearthed at Mycenae, including the exquisite gold *Mask of Agamemnon*. The German archaeologist Heinrich Schliemann found the mask placed over the face of a body that he thought was that of the legendary King Agamemnon, who died around

The Mask of Agamemnon, National Archaeological Museum

1200BC, but in fact it dates back more than 300 years earlier. In spite of this, the name remains. The prehistoric rooms also have a collection of Cycladic figures from the 3rd millennium BC. The simple, rounded female forms were funerary or devotional objects and are in contrast to the intricate pediment and frieze carvings and religious statuary from temples on the Acropolis. There is a rare male figure among the collection, and the beautiful *Harp Player* – a more complex carving in the same style.

Rooms 7–35 concentrate on sculpture – perhaps the greatest collection of ancient sculpture in the world – and this is displayed to show the chronological development of the art form. Simple, idealised male and female figures (*kouros* and *kore*) of the Archaic Age (mid-7th–5th century BC) give way to more ornate and literal human forms as you walk through the collection into the Classical Age and then on to the Hellenistic period followed by the Roman and Ptolemaic eras.

Greek gods are well represented, as are various eminent human figures of Roman times, such as a bronze statue of the Roman emperor Augustus.

Room 15 is dominated by a fine statue of Poseidon in bronze (460BC), found in the sea off the island of Évvia. The god is set to launch his trident against foes unknown. The Hall of the Stairs hosts another statue dredged from the sea, the *Jockey of the Artemision*. The diminutive jockey rides a handsome steed which has its two front legs raised into the air, as if about to leap over an invisible obstacle.

The Jockey of the Artemision

Rooms 36 to 39 contain an extraordinary collection of bronzes, including votive offerings found at the Idaean Cave in Crete – mythical birthplace of the god Zeus. Rooms 40 and 41 display artefacts from Egypt covering every era of history in the land of the Pharaohs, including the Ptolemaic period when Ptolemy (a general under Alexander the Great, and therefore of Greek descent) took control of Egypt. One of his descendants was Queen Cleopatra.

The second-floor gallery with its famous 16th-century BC wall paintings from ancient Thera (modern Santoríni), depicting everyday scenes, is one of the highlights. The paintings show such detail and the colours so vivid it's astonishing to realise how old they are.

FROM OMÓNIA TO SÝNTAGMA

Three major thoroughfares – Stadíou, Panepistimíou and Akadimías – run parallel between the Omónia area and Sýntagma Square. Stadíou has several up-market shops selling jewellery and designer labels, plus two modern stoas packed with more boutiques; these stoas were specifically mandated by the original Bavarian town plan of the 1830s and, aside from the surviving main-street grid, are its only aspect to have been faithfully adhered to.

At Paparigopoúlou 7 on the Sýntagma side of Platía Kláfthmonos you'll find the **Museum of the City of Athens** (Mon, Wed–Fri 9am–4pm, Sat–Sun 10am–3pm; charge), housed in King Otho's first residence when he arrived in Greece in 1832. Nearer to Sýntagma, on Platía Kolokotróni, is the **National Historical Museum** (Tue–Sun 9am–2pm; charge, Sun free), lodged in what was Greece's original parliament building. Its collection focuses mostly on the 1820s Greek War of Independence against Ottoman rule and the personalities involved, most of them shaggy mountain bandits recruited to the patriotic cause; an equestrian statue of one of them, Theodhore Kolokotronis, prances out front.

Neoclassical Trilogy

Northeast of Stadíou runs Panepistimíou (University Street), officially named Eleftheríou Venizélou after the Cretan-born statesman (though no one, not even official cartographers, calls it that). The location here of the **National Library**, the **University** and **National Academy** confirm it as the intellectual heart of modern Athens. All three buildings are neoclassical in design, giving an idea of how the Agora of the ancient city may have looked in its prime.

The **Academy**, on which construction work began in 1859, is the most impressive of the three. It was designed by Theophil

von Hansen, a pre-eminent architect of his generation. The seated figures of Plato and Socrates guard the entrance and an intricately carved pediment depicts the birth of Athena; all were sculpted by Leonidas Drosos. A native of Denmark, Hansen was also responsible for the the **National Library** (as well as the Záppio and Royal Observatory in Athens and a number of buildings in Vienna). Hansen's brother Christian designed the **University** in 1842; its portico, an attempted re-creation of the Parthenon's Propylaia, features frescoes of a seated King Otho flanked by the ancient Greek pantheon.

Subdued hues

The Hansen-designed Academy, National Library (above) and University are faithful reproductions of Classical architecture in all but one respect: colour. Flecks of paint on particularly well-preserved ancient artefacts tell us that neon-garish blues, reds, oranges and yellows were the rule for ancient statuary and relief work, but this was apparently felt to be too vulgar for modern sensibilities, so the pediments are in more subdued hues.

Continuing towards Sýntagma you will pass the Renaissance-style home of the archaeologist Heinrich Schliemann, who was instrumental in turning the myth of the Mycenaeans and the Trojan War into fact. Today it houses the **Numismatic Museum** (Panepistimíou 12; Tue–Sun 8.30am–3pm; charge), containing an extraordinary collection of 600,000 coins from antiquity to modern times.

The northeasternmost thoroughfare is Akadimías, which runs behind the Library, University and Academy. Behind these buildings at Akadimías 50 is the Athens Cultural Centre, housing the **Theatre Museum** (Mon 11am–7pm, Tue–Sun 8am–7pm; free), with displays of the Greek theatrical world. Beyond Akadimías in the same direction lies **Exárhia**, the traditional locus of book stores and book publishing, and the student quarter with its multicoloured graffiti and posters boosting every contrarian cause.

SÝNTAGMA SQUARE AND AROUND

Platía Syntágmatos (Constitution Square) is dominated on the west by the imposing façade of the **Parliament Building** (Voulí), originally built as the royal palace and completed in 1842. The west face, facing the square, has a

A pedestrianised section of Sýntagma Square

Doric portico made of Pentelic marble. In front of the building on the retaining wall is the **Memorial of the Unknown Soldier**, commemorating all Greeks who have fallen in war. Decorated with a modern carved relief of a Classical theme, the marble is inscribed with an oration by Pericles honouring the Peloponnesian War dead. *Évzones* – traditionally dressed soldiers – guard the tomb and the presidential residence on Iródou Attikoú. The formal **'changing of the guard'** takes place every Sunday at 10.45am; however, the *évzones* have a duty-changeover every hour during the day when two new guards take the place of the previous shift. This is one activity that you should not miss on your trip to Athens.

The **Grande Bretagne Hotel** on the northeast corner of the square was also built in 1842 as a sumptuous private residence and has become an Athenian institution. During World War II it became the military headquarters of both the Germans and the British. Winston Churchill survived a thwarted bomb-plot here during his stay in December 1944. Thoroughly renovated before the 2004 Olympics, it is worth stopping in at the Grande Bretagne for a drink at the Alexander Bar (dress properly!).

The Grande Bretagne Hotel

Around Sýntagma

Just behind the Parliament building are the verdant landscaped grounds of the **National Gardens** (sunrise–sunset; free), conceived by King Otho's queen, Amalia, and an oasis with artificial streams and duck ponds. Just south of the garden is the **Záppeio**, an imposing neoclassical building designed by Theophil von Hansen as a national exhibition centre in 1878, set in its own gardens (24hr). It now houses a modern conference centre, with a popular (if pricey) café adjacent.

A five-minute stroll from Sýntagma along Amalías (or through the National Gardens) to the junction with Vassilís Ólgas brings you to another ancient site, **Hadrian's Arch**, built by the Athenians for the emperor Hadrian in AD131–2. The west side of the arch facing the Acropolis and the ancient agoras bears an inscription reading, 'This is Athens, the former city of Theseus'. The inscription on the other side reads 'This is the city of Hadrian and not of Theseus'.

Immediately east looms the **Temple of Olympian Zeus** (daily Apr–Oct 8am–7.30pm, Nov–Mar 8am–5pm; charge or included in Acropolis ticket), the largest temple ever built on Greek soil. Work began on this colossal temple in the 6th century BC, but was only completed 650 years later. Hadrian dedicated the temple to the ruler of the ancient pantheon, Zeus Olym-

Cats' home

The National Gardens *(above)* are home to large colonies of semi-feral, abandoned cats. Local animal welfare organisations attempt to look after them, find homes for them, and alleviate periodic spates of poisonings.

Lykavittós

Northeast of the Sýntagma area rises the steep, pine-covered hill of Lykavittós, which unlike Filopáppos and Ardittós was not settled or used much in ancient times owing to a lack of water supply. Today it is topped by the chapel of Ágios Geórgios and a rather over-priced restaurant. Both can be reached either by an arduous walk up from the posh Kolonáki residential district at the foot of the hill, or by the funicular from the corner of Aristíppou and Ploutárhou (every 30 minutes).

pios, during the Panathenaic Festival in AD131–2. It was imperative that the temple should be fitting for his position, and its dimensions – 96m (315ft) long and 40m (130ft) wide, with columns more than 17m (53ft) high – are truly majestic. Originally 104 columns surrounded an inner sanctum that protected a gold-and-ivory statue of Zeus which has since been lost. Today only 16 columns are still standing, but their Corinthian capitals have a wonderful form and elegance.

The temple sat close to the banks of the River Ilissos in ancient times and near the fountain of Kallirrhoe, whose lush vegetation created an even more beautiful vista. Today the river has been covered over and lies beneath a busy boulevard. Nearby, along Vassilísis Ólgas, is the **Panathenaïkó Stadium**, sitting in the lee of Ardittós Hill. The stadium was first constructed in 330–329BC for the ancient Panathenaic Games. It was rebuilt by the city's great benefactor, Herodes Atticus, in AD140. A modern Greek benefactor, George Averoff, sponsored the stadium's reconstruction for the first modern Olympic Games, held here in 1896. However, the length is too short and the turns too tight for modern athletic events, so the 2004 Olympic Games were staged primarily at a purpose-built Olympic complex in the northern suburb of Maroússi.

Leading directly east from Sýntagma Square is Avenue Vassilísis Sofías. This main thoroughfare, with a number of major embassies on or just off it, leads to several important museums, all within walking distance or near the Evangelismós metro station.

Closest to Sýntagma is the **Benaki Museum** (Koumbári 1; Mon, Wed–Sat 9am–5pm, Thur until midnight, Sun 9am–3pm; charge but free Thur), a collection donated to the state in 1954 by the wealthy cotton merchant Emmanouil Benakis, who was born in the Greek community of Alexandria. Since its renovation in 2000, this main building of the Benaki Museum has focused almost exclusively on Greece. It is probably the only museum that covers all ages of Greek culture and history, and there are Greek works of art from prehistoric to modern times. The museum also has an excellent gift shop and a very popular roof café.

The peak of Lykavittós Hill looming 277m (910ft) above the city

A Cycladic figurine

Three blocks over from Sýntagma is the **Goulandrís Museum of Cycladic Art** (Neofýtou Douká 4; Mon, Wed–Fri 10am–4pm, Thur until 8pm, Sat 10am–3pm; charge). This museum celebrates the art discovered in the Cyclades islands (*c*.3000–2000BC). Most of the exquisite marble figures are female, suggesting the worship of fertility or an earth-mother religion. The museum also holds around 300 objects dating from Classical, Hellenic and Roman Greece, including a collection of fine bronze vessels.

Further down Vassilísis Sofías is the newly extended **Byzantine and Christian Museum** (Tue–Sun 7.30am–7.30pm; charge). One of the original buildings here is a splendid 19th-century mansion built for the eccentric Philhellene Duchesse de Plaisance (1785–1854), who was married to one of Napoleon's generals but came to Greece, fell in love with the country, and stayed. The mansion is now overshadowed by the huge and impressive new underground wing, which houses the bulk of this collection of artefacts from the early Christian period and right through the Byzantine era. Despite being underground the large rooms are light and spacious, and the beautiful objects well-displayed and informatively labelled. This stylish transformation has made what was once a small and specialist collection into one of the major Athens museums.

Next door to the Byzantine Museum is the **War Museum** (Tue–Sun 9am–2pm; free), established during the 1967–74 dictatorship. Outside stand World War II tanks and aeroplanes, and the galleries inside display historic uniforms, armour and hand-held weapons. The upper floors are devoted to military tactics and battle plans, examining campaigns from ancient times to World War II.

Beyond Evangelismós metro station, opposite the Hilton Hotel, is the **National Gallery** (Mon, Wed, Thur, Fri, Sat 9am–3pm, Mon, Wed 6–9pm, Sun 10am–2pm; charge). The core collection of Greek art from the 16th century to the present is mostly post-Byzantine icons and canvases; highlights include some El Grecos and the works of Nikos-Hatzikyriakos Ghikas (Ghika), active during much of the 20th century.

EXCURSIONS

Athens is undeniably a fascinating city, but with the traffic and congestion, even the listed attractions can begin to pall after a few days. Luckily you are perfectly placed to take in numerous excursions for the day or even a few days, either on an organised tour or under your own steam.

Monastery of Kessarianí

Nestled in a vale on the slopes of Mount Imittós 5km (3 miles) east of the city centre, the monastery at **Kessarianí** (Tue–Sun 8.30am–3pm; charge) and its surrounding gardens are a favourite retreat of city-dwellers. The River Ilissos rises here, nourishing the vegetation which has been a constant since ancient times; gently graded hiking trails loop through the gardens and further into the wilderness of Pendéli. The monastery compound itself encloses a refectory, Byzantine baths and the original 11th-century church, decorated with vivid frescoes from 1682 of scenes from the life of Christ.

Monastery of Dáfni

The ancient Sacred Way or Ierá Odós *(see box, page 49)* –
now traced more or less exactly by the modern boulevard of
the same name – heads west from Kerameikos through modest residential quarters to the edge of the city, in Haïdári district. Here in a wooded pass, 10km (6 miles) from the centre,
sits the **Monastery of Dáfni**, built on the site of an earlier
temple of Apollo.

The original monastery founded here in the 5th or 6th century was lavishly refurbished in 1070, when the impressive
mosaics were installed. From 1207 until 1458, when Athens
was ruled by Frankish lords, the monastery was occupied by
Cistercian monks. Certain reoccupation of the monastery by
Orthodox monks can be dated only to the early 16th century, and they were expelled during the 1820s for harbouring
independence fighters. Restoration took place after World
War II, again in the 1960s, and yet again since 1999 when
the last Athens earthquake caused severe damage. The pretty Byzantine church has a stone-and-tile dome exterior and
is renowned throughout Greece for its beautiful mosaics, particularly that of *Christ Pantokrator* in the main dome.

Ancient Eleusis

Continuing along the Sacred Way, which in ancient times was
lined with shrines and tombs, brings you to an industrial
landscape of shipyards, steel foundries and oil refineries on
the Saronic Gulf – amidst which, incongruously, is one of the
most hallowed sites of the ancient world: ancient **Eleusis**
(Tue–Sun 8.30am–3pm; charge), marooned beside decided-
ly unromantic **modern Elefsína**.

Eleusis, actually a small town, was home to the Sanctuary
of Demeter and the Eleusian Mysteries – a series of complex
and enigmatic rituals performed by priests of the order before
an audience of male, non-slave citizens. The Mysteries thrived

Yachts and fishing boats, Piraeus

from the Mycenaean era to the coming of Christianity, but the exact nature of the rites was never divulged, as all initiates kept – on pain of death – the secrets of the cult. Eleusis has suffered badly over the centuries, and the excellent site museum with finds and models of the sanctuary helps make sense of what today is largely an expanse of jumbled masonry.

Piraeus

Just 10km (6 miles) southwest of Athens' centre, and almost indistinguishable from the sprawling capital, is Piraeus (Piréas). This metropolis of almost half a million people is actually the third-largest city in Greece, and the country's largest port. Although most people just use Piraeus as a departure point for the Aegean islands, the city has a few of its own attractions. Coming from central Athens, the metro brings you to within walking distance of the water, where the half-dozen distinct quays or aktés on the main harbour

Bronze gods

Just west of Zéa is the Archaeological Museum of Piraeus (Tue–Sun 8.30am–3pm; charge). This rather dour building hides a treasure trove of artefacts found during local excavations – or dredged by chance from the sea bed nearby. Pride of place goes to a 6th-century BC life-sized bronze of Apollo, displayed along with similar statues of Artemis and Athena.

accommodate dozens of ferries, catamarans and hydrofoils. From Aktí Miaoúli any street heading south leads to pretty **Zéa marina** (formerly Pashálimani), the second of Piraeus' three natural harbours, crammed with enormous fibreglass pleasure craft and smaller yachts. Aktí Moutsopoúlou, lined with expensive fish restaurants, loops around the bay. Still further east is **Mikrolímano**, home to more boats and pleasant cafés.

The Saronic Gulf Islands

The islands closest to Athens are those of the Saronic Gulf: Égina (Aegina), Póros, Ýdra (Hydra) and Spétses. The nearest is 45 minutes by hydrofoil from Piraeus. Hydrofoils for these islands depart from Aktí Miaoúli at Piraeus; slower ferries just opposite from Aktí Poseidónos. Note that there are very few connections between Égina and the other islands.

Égina (Aegina)

This is the closest island to the mainland, and the pretty quayside of **Égina (Aegina) town**, with its neoclassical buildings, awaits as you disembark near the whitewashed chapel of Ágios Nikólaos, protecting the harbour entrance. Walk along the water's edge past the colourful fishing fleet, have lunch at a taverna in the marketplace or buy some of the pistachio nuts for which the island is renowned. Égina is a delight out of season, but can be very busy at weekends, especially in summer. Many houses here are second homes for wealthy Athenian families. The resort of **Agía Marína** is 15km (9 miles) from the town on the east coast and has a good, child-friendly beach. Just before, stop off at the 5th-century BC **Temple of Aphaia**, set on a hilltop amidst pines.

Póros

Volcanic Póros lies less than 150m (465ft) from the Greek mainland, off the northeastern coast of the Argolid Peninsula and an hour from Piraeus by hydrofoil. Small sailing boats throng the narrow straits, a yachtsman's paradise in the summer months. **Póros town** – the only settlement on the island – is a maze of narrow winding streets rising up a small hill with a clock tower. The seafront is the hub of all activity, with tavernas and cafés lining the waterside. The rest of Póros is covered with verdant pine forest, while the coastline is dotted with small rocky coves – great for swimming and snorkelling.

The harbour of Póros town

The only other sights are the **monastery of Zoödóhou Pigís**, east of town, and the foundations of a **temple to Poseidon** well inland near the top of the island. Here the famous Greek orator Demosthenes chose suicide in 322BC rather than surrender to Macedonian forces.

Ýdra (Hydra)

Just over an hour and a half from Athens by hydrofoil, Ýdra (Hydra) is the most celebrated of the Saronic Gulf islands, and the approach into its harbour the most dramatic. The beautiful port of **Ýdra town** remains hidden until the very last moment, and when the panorama comes into view your camera should be ready. Above the narrow cove the hillsides are blanketed with neoclassical mansions. There are no cars on Ýdra except for the odd rubbish truck and mechanical digger, only donkeys which transport almost everything up the slopes. There are very few beaches, but the water is very clear for snorkelling, and there is some excellent walking.

Still, most people don't visit Ýdra for any activity other than to 'see and be seen'. During the 1950s and 1960s the island was an artist colony, though today it has developed into an upscale resort. Pricey jewellery boutiques intermingle with craft galleries, exclusive restaurants, surprisingly inexpensive Greek tavernas and chic cafés. At busy times, evening hydrofoils back to Piraeus often fill quickly so buy a return ticket in Piraeus or see to it immediately upon arrival at Ýdra.

Spétses

At well over two hours away from Piraeus by hydrofoil, Spétses is the remotest of the Saronic Gulf islands and just a bit too far to do as a day-trip. The town, while not as immediately striking as Ýdra's, has a similar architecture and straggles pleasantly along the north coast for several kilometres. Unlike Ýdra, motorised vehicles are not totally banned on Spétses, though private cars are prohibited in the town itself – horse-drawn buggies, scooters and a few conventional taxis are the main alternatives. Away from town, Spétses has the best beaches and cleanest water of any Saronic Gulf island, best explored by hired boat or scooter.

Sounion

The peninsula of southern Attica reaches out towards the Aegean Sea, and at its most windswept tip the ancient Greeks built a beautiful **Temple to Poseidon** (daily 10am–sunset; charge), the god of the sea, earthquakes and horses. The views from here are beautiful whatever the time of day – but the sunsets are particularly spectacular. The temple itself is one of the finest in Greece. Of the 34 Doric columns only 16 are still in situ, and the ornate frieze on the pediment and entablature has been ravaged by the salty air, but the whole effect of the building combined with the setting – a sandy beach on one side and a sheer drop on the other – is magnificent.

Sounion is reached by following the coast road from the capital 70km (43 miles) southeast through several resort-suburbs with both fee-payable and free beaches.

The Temple of Poseidon at Sounion

Corinth

The history of ancient Greece is punctuated with the feats of city-states led by great leaders, of which Athens is, of course, the most famous. Within a day's journey of the capital lies the **Argolid Peninsula**, a region of the Peloponnese, where the sites of two such city-states – Corinth and Mycenae – can be viewed. Those with more time should definitely visit the ancient Theatre of Epidauros and the port city of Náfplio.

The Corinth Canal

An engineering marvel, the **Corinth Canal** cuts the narrow isthmus that links the Peloponnese with the Greek mainland and divides the Saronic Gulf from the Gulf of Corinth. Sailing around the Peloponnese took considerable time and exposed ships to some of the most dangerous waters in the Mediterranean – especially in winter. Ancient Greeks ported their huge vessels across the 6km (4-mile) wide isthmus, and as early as AD67, the Roman Emperor Nero was making the first attempts at cutting a canal. It would not become a reality until 1893 when, after 11 years of digging, a channel was opened for shipping. Its modest dimensions, however, made it obsolete almost immediately, even more so in the contemporary era of supertankers.

The Corinth Canal

Ancient Corinth

In ancient times Corinth rivalled Athens in its power and influence. It mimicked the layout of the larger city – a town radiated out from the base of a rocky pinnacle which housed a temple of Aphrodite – though Acrocorinth is much higher than the Acropolis.

Corinth was an active and prosperous city from the 8th to the 5th centuries BC, founding many colonies and competing fiercely with Athens; it sided with Sparta against Athens in the Peloponnesian Wars (431–404BC). During the Hellenistic period the city was economically prosperous despite political instability. After 224BC when the Achaean League was formed, Corinth became a centre of independent Greek political life. This brought it into direct conflict with Rome, which razed Corinth to the ground in 146BC.

The site was unoccupied for just over 100 years, until Julius Caesar began to rebuild the city in 44BC. Revitalised, Corinth soon became the capital of the Roman province of Achaea and the seat of the Roman consul. The city developed its two ports (Kenchreai to the east and Lechaion to the west of the isthmus) and was flourishing when St Paul arrived on his first visit to Corinth in AD50/51, when he successfully established a community of believers.

In the 3rd and 4th centuries Corinth suffered attacks by the Goths and a major earthquake in 375. During the 6th century there were more earthquakes and Slavic invasions of the Peloponnese, after which the city was abandoned.

The modern and uninteresting city of Corinth lies several kilometres northeast of the site, leaving **ancient Corinth** (summer 8am–8pm, winter 8am–3pm; charge) for us to explore. Most prominent as you approach the site is the Doric **Temple of Apollo**, built in the 6th century BC and one of the oldest buildings in Corinth. Many other remains date from the Roman era, including ornate façades of the **Fountain of**

Peirene, where you can still hear the waters flowing through cavities at the rear, and the **Lechaion Way**, with worn cart tracks clearly visible in the marble slabs.

The **Bema** (platform), traditionally believed to be the site where St Paul stood before the Roman consul, is situated to the south side of the agora. The site **museum** contains some interesting finds and features a number of dioramas depicting Corinth as it would once have looked.

After visiting the ancient city, head up the hill to take in the magnificent site of **Acrocorinth** standing sentinel above. Fortified since the 7th century BC, the summit is encircled by high stone walls which were continually reinforced during the Byzantine and Ottoman eras. At the summit, within three layers of protective walls, are the remains of a Temple of Aphrodite, an early Christian basilica, Byzantine cisterns, a Frankish tower and Ottoman mosques and fountains.

Mycenae

From the 15th to the 11th century BC, this rocky outcrop was one of the most important centres in the known world, seat of the mighty Mycenaean empire which grew to encompass mainland Greece and the northern Aegean islands. The exploits of the Mycenaeans, and their greatest leader Agamemnon, were thought to be myth until – in the 1870s – the German archaeologist Heinrich Schliemann set out to find evidence of Homer's stories in (until then) strictly legendary Troy and Mycenae. He successfully uncovered both sites, and thereby transformed the world of archaeology – and man's view of history.

Schliemann found the remains of the city of **Mycenae** (daily summer 8am–7pm, winter 8am–5pm; charge) buried under thousands of years' worth of debris in a sheltered valley some 60km (37 miles) south of Corinth. It was so well hidden that the site had been completely forgotten, and surprisingly it had not been plundered by robbers.

The military might of the Mycenaeans had been well documented by Homer, but nothing could prepare Schliemann's team for the artistic treasures unearthed here. As they dug through the remains, the tombs of several kings were discovered; each skeleton lay where it had been carefully buried, its face covered in a mask of pure gold. Exquisite statuary and intricate jewellery found in the family tombs below show a softer side of these enigmatic people and bring the world of Agamemnon to life. All the artefacts from the site were taken to Athens and many are now on display in the

The Lion's Gate, erected in the 13th century BC

National Archaeological Museum *(see page 54)*.

The site's massive **Cyclopean walls** – huge rough-hewn masonry blocks laid atop one another with extreme precision, and without mortar – are so called because later Hellenes could not believe that humans were responsible for the construction and so gave the credit to the one-eyed giant of myth. The outer walls, which measured up to 14m (46ft) wide, date from around 1250BC; they surround and protect the citadel through which the only entrance is the **Lion's Gate**, decorated with the earliest known monumental sculpture in Europe.

Just beyond the gate, look down to the right to see **Grave Circle A**, where the royal graves were found, then

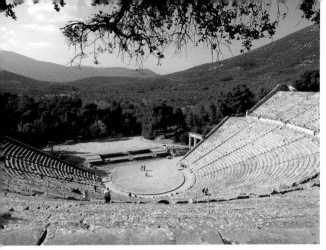

The ancient Theatre of Epidauros

climb to the top of the settlement to the remains of the Royal Palace, from where the views of the surrounding countryside are superb. Outside the walls are three *tholos* (beehive) tombs, including the **Treasury of Atreus**, otherwise known as the **Tomb of Agamemnon**, built in about 1330BC. The masonry – again eschewing the use of mortar – is superb, as is the reverberating echo which is irresistible to noisy school children.

Epidauros

Southeast of Mycenae, some 40 minutes' drive via the beautiful city of Náfplio, is another ancient site also renowned for its acoustics. The extraordinarily well-preserved **Theatre of Epidauros** (Epídavros; daily summer 8am–7pm, winter 8am–5pm) was built in the late 4th century BC and could accommodate an audience of 12,000 people. It has startling acoustics: you may not hear the proverbial pin drop in the centre of the stage while you are sitting in an upper row, but you can certainly hear quiet speech. Performances are staged here every summer, as part of the **Hellenic Festival** *(see page 82)*. The theatre was part of a much larger **Sanctuary of Asklepion**, one of the most important centres of healing in the ancient world.

Náfplio

The port town of **Náfplio** makes the perfect base for touring the area, or perhaps a spot to have lunch while on a daytrip. Set on the south coast of the Argolid, it has been a strategic strongpoint for centuries and has no less than three castles dating from Byzantine and Venetian times on the towering rock of Palamídi, plus a fourth on the rock of Akronafplía. The city retains much of its Venetian and Ottoman past, and served as the capital of the newly independent state from 1829 until 1834. Here, also, the first president of independent Greece, Ioánnis Kapodístrias, was assassinated in 1831.

Many tavernas set out tables in the lanes of the architecturally protected old town, and tempt you with fresh seafood landed by the small fishing boats in the harbour. The seaside promenade flanked by smart cafés is where you will find locals and Athenians alike strolling in the cooling evening air. Look out towards the tiny fortified island of **Boúrtzi**; the Venetian castle there has variously been the residence of the town's executioner and a luxury hotel.

Náfplio harbour

The Tholos, Delphi

Delphi

The advice of the oracle at **Delphi** (daily summer 8am–7.30pm, winter 8.30am–3pm; charge) was available to all who were willing to make the pilgrimage to the Sanctuary of Apollo, nowadays a three-hour journey on a modern road from Athens, on the flanks of Mount Parnassós.

In ancient times Delphi was the spiritual centre of the Greek world, and no important decisions of state were made without consulting the oracle here. The cult flourished from the 8th century BC to the 4th century AD. The resident priestess or *Pythia* was a woman in her fifties who sat on a tripod inside the Temple of Apollo, periodically falling into a trance when Apollo would enter her as his medium. Her unintelligible mutterings were interpreted by the temple priests, who in turn would give often ambiguous answers to the supplicants.

A modern road cuts through the ancient remains, and the approach to the site from the parking area leads up a sacred way, past many treasuries and offerings dedicated by various city-states, to the magnificent **Temple of Apollo**, which has been partly reconstructed by French archaeologists. About 400m (1,300ft) east are the waters of the **Kastalian Spring**, where pilgrims would purify themselves before consulting the Pythia. Just below the road and the spring are the remains of a large gymnasium used by athletes competing in the Pythian Games, and the temple of **Athena Pronaia**, where pilgrims would make their first religious stop on the climb to the sanctuary. The most impressive building at this lower site, of uncertain function, is the circular **Tholos**, built in black-and-white stone. The local **museum** displays an extraordinary collection of statuary and other artefacts found at the site, the most famous exhibit being the 5th-century BC bronze statue of the **Charioteer**. Other items include two enormous 6th-century BC *kouroi*, and a life-sized votive bull fashioned from hammered silver and copper.

Aráhova

Eleven kilometres (7 miles) east of Delphi, the road from Athens passes through the town of Aráhova on the slopes of **Mount Parnassós**. Teeming in winter with skiers from the two nearby **ski resorts** of Kelária and Fterólakka (23km/15 miles and 29km/18 miles away respectively), the town feels somewhat quieter during the summer months, though it makes an excellent base for mountain hikes in the area.

Osios Loukás Monastery

Located just 24km (15 miles) southwest of Aráhova along a minor road, the **Monastery of Osios Loukás** (daily summer 8am–2pm and 4–7pm, winter 8am–5pm; charge) is considered to be one of the finest Byzantine buildings in Greece and it is well worth the pilgrimage to see its stunning frescoes and mosaics.

Mosaic depicting Osios Loukás

WHAT TO DO

ENTERTAINMENT

Athens comes alive after dark with a range of activities; however, you'll probably need to alter your normal routine to enjoy it as the locals do. Theatre or cinema performances are followed by a late leisurely dinner, often after 11pm, and musical nightclub performances begin at around midnight. Even if you only want to sample the delights of Greek tavernas and perhaps stroll around Pláka, the real atmosphere accrues after 9pm when local families dine out.

For most Greeks, the traditional taverna – eating, drinking and often singing with friends – is the favoured choice for a night out. Other options include bars *(barákia)*, especially in Psyrrí and Exárhia districts; live music clubs with jazz, Greek music or rock; dance clubs with a techno, house or ambient soundtrack; and musical tavernas where the price of the food on offer reflects the live entertainment.

Theatre, Cinema and Music

The ancient Greeks were credited with inventing drama and comedy, and this tradition carries on into the present. The city has over a hundred active **theatres** at peak winter times, though the season lasts from October to May, and you might make a special effort to see a play in the magnificent theatre at Epidauros *(see page 76)*. All performances are in Greek. From late May to mid-September, **open-air cinemas** operate in most neighbourhoods. Screenings are typically at 9pm and 11pm, and films – usually from the preceding winter – are subtitled, with the original soundtrack.

The Theatre of Herodes Atticus at night

From October to May a full programme of classical music is at the **Mégaro Mousikís** (Athens Concert Hall; tel: 210 72 82 333; www.megaron.gr). The **Lyriki Skini** or national opera company in the Olympia Theatre (Akadimías 59–61; tel: 210 36 11 516) has opera and musicals at the same time.

Summer Festival

The **Hellenic Festival** (widely mis-dubbed the 'Athens Festival') runs from mid-May to late September, with a full programme of cultural events including choral concerts, dance and recitals. Performances are aimed at both visitors and Athenians, and tickets are fairly priced. Since 1955 they have been staged at the atmospheric open-air **Herodes Atticus** theatre below the Acropolis, with world-class performers both foreign and Greek. The festival has grown so much since the late 1980s that a second venue, the **Lykavittós Theatre** on the eponymous hill, handles nearly as many events. On weekend nights during July and August the ancient theatre of Epidauros stages ancient Greek plays presented in modern Greek.

For information about all festival productions, contact the box office at Panepistimíou 39, in the arcade (tel: 210 32 21 459 or 210 92 82 900; www.greekfestival.gr), or the Herodes Atticus box office on the day of the performance from 6–9pm (tel: 210 32 32 771). Big-name events sell out quickly, so make this a priority upon arrival in Athens. The Lykavittós Theatre is contactable on tel: 210 72 27 233.

The **Vyronas Festival** runs for six weeks from July to September at the Théatro Vráhon 'Melina Mercouri' in the suburb of Výronas, attracting a mix of jazz, rock, ethnic and Greek acts (for current information tel: 210 76 55 748 or 210 76 62 066). Two other, smaller events in early summer are also worth catching: the **Glyfáda Festival** at the Exoni Theatre on Ydras 11, with events in an abandoned quarry at the foot of Mt Pendéli (tel: 210 89 12 200), and the Rematia Festival at the Rematia Theatre in the northern suburb of Halándri (tel: 210 68 00 001).

Traditional Music and Dance

Greece has a rich legacy of folk dance and music; however, genuine, spontaneous performances are hard to find in the capital.

From late May to late September the **Dóra Strátou Folk Dance Theatre** presents stagings of traditional Greek song, dance and music in its own open-air theatre

Music accompanies a meal

opposite the Acropolis on Filopáppos Hill (daily except Mon; for details and tickets tel: 210 32 44 395).

SPORTS

Athens' proximity to the coast offers opportunities to combine **beach activities** with a city holiday, with some excellent facilities within a 30-minute taxi or bus ride of the centre. You'll find a full range of sports on offer, from tennis, windsurfing and waterskiing to snorkelling and scuba. However, the submarine world near the capital can be disappointing, and the water is not generally considered clean enough for bathing anywhere north of Glyfáda.

Much of Athens closes down during August (though not those businesses relating to tourism), when people head to the coast, the mountains or the islands. **Beaches** are busy throughout the school holidays, which run from mid-June to early September. The closest resort to the centre is **Glyfáda**, only 12km (7 miles) away. About 20km (12 miles) distant is **Voúla**, a bit less crowded than Glyfáda. **Vouliagméni** is 5km (3 miles) further south, while **Várkiza** lies another 5km (3 miles) further still, at the end of city bus lines. There are some luxurious hotels in both Voúla and Vouliagméni, and each of these resorts has at least one beach with changing facilities, food and watersports. An entrance fee of about €5 is typical.

The **Saronic Gulf islands** have a longer season, from April to October, owing to foreigner patronage. Égina (Aegina) does not have the best sea; you'll want to go to its little satellite Angístri for swimming. Ýdra and Spétses generally have clean water and are the best organised for watersports.

Sailing

Summer **sailing** is very popular with Athenians as the crowded marinas at Piraeus, Álimos and Glyfáda all testify. Competitions are held regularly all summer, and even children have their own events. Several companies hire boats with crew, or 'bare' if you have a skipper's certificate. Try, for example, Fyly Yachting and Partners at Poseidónos 73, Kalamáki (tel: 210 98 58 670; www.fyly.gr), or MG Yachts, also in Kalamáki at Makáriou 2 (tel: 210 98 59 101; www.mgyachts.gr).

Skiing

Skiing facilities can be found at **Mount Parnassós** *(see page 79)*, nearly three hours' drive from the city, where there are 20 or so mostly intermediate runs open from December to April. The hotels and tavernas of modern Delfí and Aráhova lie 20 minutes from the slopes if you want a village atmosphere; Aráhova is also full of outfitters for renting or buying equipment. These – and lift passes – are comparable in cost to that of northern Europe.

Football (Soccer)

Football is a national obsession in Greece, and Athens' teams (Panathinaïkós and AEKAthens), plus Olympiakós of Piraeus, feature prominently in domestic and European competition.

The season runs from September to May, with matches on Wednesday nights and Saturday afternoons. Both AEK and Panathinaïkós play at the Olympic Stadium in Maroússi. This is only a temporary arrangement while both teams have new stadiums built, so check for details. Olympiakós' Kariskáki stadium is in Néo Fáliro. Ask hotel reception for assistance in obtaining match tickets.

SHOPPING

Athens offers an array of shopping opportunities, not only for typical Greek-style souvenirs, but for haute couture, art and jewellery. Whatever your budget, you are bound to find something exciting to take home – whether a mass-produced item or a unique hand-finished piece. Individual districts specialise in certain types of goods.

Shopping for icons

Where to Shop

For undeniably touristy, mass-produced kitsch, head for **Pláka**, where such outlets are interspersed with galleries, T-shirt shops and numerous street hawkers selling fun toys or handmade budget art. The maze of streets around the cathedral offers religious souvenirs – incense burners, icons and *támata* (votive offerings) being the most portable.

Monastiráki is Athens' old bazaar area; at the Sunday **flea market** on and around Platía Avyssinías *(see page 50)* you can find old metalware, dishes, memorabilia and furniture – and an array of small shops on Iféstou sells everything from used CDs and beads to army-surplus-type clothing. The covered **Varvákio market** *(see page 53)* between Athinás and Eólou offers a range of Greek foodstuffs to take home.

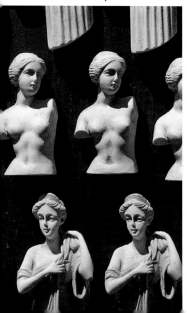

Reproductions of ancient Greek statuary

The **Kolonáki** district is an Athenian favourite for boutiques and home furnishing stores selling the best of European design; prices match (and even exceed) quality here. Ermoú, Eólou and Stadíou streets are where you will find more middle-of-the-road shops selling everything from shoes and clothing to household wares. There are also Greek department stores such as Fokas (Ermoú 11) and Notos (Eólov 2–8).

What to Buy

Copper and brassware.
Copper and brass have long
been used for household
utensils, and skilled crafts-
men still work in small, central workshops. Newly made
goods have a bright patina
that mellows with age; some
of the older pieces – including water urns, bowls and
covered pilaf pots – are exceptionally beautiful. Ornate

Dodgy deals

Prices are fixed everywhere
but the flea market, so that's
the only place you can really
haggle. If you find a deal that
is too good to be true for
ancient coins, they're probably fakes. Bear in mind that
if they're real you're not
supposed to take them out
of the country anyway. The
same applies to all antiquities (see page 109).

Ottoman-style trays (siniá) set on folding wooden bases will
just fit in your luggage, as will serving ladles and goats' bells.
The best sources of antique copperware are several shops at
the far end of Adrianoú opposite the Stoa of Attalos, and
stalls on Platía Avyssinías. New copperware is sold at a few
shops on Iféstou. None of it is especially cheap, but hard bar-
gaining at slow times can yield fair prices.

Ceramics. Exquisite hand-thrown and painted copies of
ancient pieces are available at a price, though you can also
buy numerous examples of less expensive factory-produced
items. Traditionally shaped urns, jugs and cups are decorated with scenes depicting the lives of ancient mortals or the
Greek gods. Modern ceramic artists also thrive, and many
small galleries showcase hand-created pieces.

Statuary. If you want a (reproduction) little piece of ancient Greece then you will have no trouble finding your own
copy of a deity or a Classical statue. Plaques depicting ancient friezes or masks to hang on walls are also extremely
popular, as are Mycenaean helmets.

If Classical statuary is too ornate for your taste, then
copies of the minimalist Cycladic idols are to be found at the

Goulandrís Museum of Cycladic Art. Similarly, both the Benáki Museum and National Archaeological Museum offer high-quality copies of items from their collection. Each comes with a certificate of authentication.

Leatherware. Goat- and cow-hides are worked into a range of footwear, bags and clothing, though quality is generally more rustic and bohemian than similar items produced in Italy or France.

Carpets and needlepoint. The carpet-weaving tradition was largely introduced by Asia Minor refugees. Look for hand-knotted ornate patterns in wool or silk, which come with a hefty price tag. Hand-produced *flokáti* rugs made from sheep hides were used in farmhouses on the mainland.

Needlepoint, crochet and embroidery – once activities undertaken by every Greek woman – are dying arts, so any hand-crafted pieces will become collectors' items. Machine-produced pieces are readily available in the form of table-cloths, napkins, cushion covers and handkerchiefs.

Jewellery. Greece has been renowned since ancient times for its worksmanship in gold and silver, and many high-class

Amulets to ward off the evil eye

jewellery stores in Athens still produce superb-quality items. Athenian women love to adorn themselves with these metals, and with precious stones imported from elsewhere. Prices are very competitive as gold is sold by weight, with a relatively small mark-up for the craftsman's skill. Many items incorporate traditional designs that have changed little since ancient times. The major museums also sell copies of popular exhibits.

Although not strictly speaking jewellery, worry beads or *kombolói* – carried by many Greek men of the older generation to calm the nerves – are extremely decorative. The best worry beads feature cornelian or amber, with silver decoration and silk thread.

Icons. These are religious portraits, usually of a saint or sacred event. At the heart of Orthodox worship, they serve as a focus of prayer and a window to the divine.

For centuries icons were popular souvenirs of a grand European tour or religious

Greek worry beads

pilgrimage. However, modern production methods, involving the use of thin artificial canvas and gaudy synthetic colours, reduced their popularity. In recent years, however, there has been a rebirth of traditional icon-painting methods, both in church renovations and commercially. Natural pigments and egg tempura binding are painstakingly mixed and applied to a canvas bound over wood. Gold leaf is then applied and the image is given a patina. This time-consuming work is exquisite and expensive.

Pre-1821 icons will require an export permit. You will find mass-produced icons in many tourist shops, but for quality pieces it is worth paying a visit to a specialist store or to the shop of the Byzantine Museum.

Edibles and drinks. Non-perishable foodstuffs from the Greek countryside include honey, herbs, olives and olive oil, pasta like *hilópites* or *trahanás*, and pine nuts or almonds. For an alcoholic souvenir, try *oúzo* – the aniseed-flavoured national aperitif – or Greek brandy, which is slightly sweeter than French cognac. Metaxa is a special brand invented by a silk trader named Spyros Metaxas; its star rating denotes its age.

Bottles in the Brettos liquor store, a Pláka institution

CHILDREN'S ATHENS

Athens requires some forethought if you are taking young children. Not all will be eager to spend days at the ruins, and the weather can be oppressively hot during the summer. However, children will be welcomed almost everywhere they go.

Eminently children-friendly are the National Gardens *(see page 61)* with their duck ponds and playground, and also the Pédion Áreos, near the National Archaeological Museum, which has play facilities. The Children's Museum *(see page 41)* in Pláka is similarly geared towards play, with lots to build, paint and deconstruct (overalls provided).

Alternatively, a boat trip to one of the nearby islands makes a wonderful day's outing *(see pages 68–70)*, with numerous destinations only one or two hours away by hydrofoil or ferry. If all else fails, a day at the beach should blow the city cobwebs away *(see pages 83–4)*.

Calendar of Events

1 January: Protohroniá or St Basil's Day, a time of parties and gifts; the traditional greeting is *Kalí Hroniá*, and cakes *(vassilópita)* are eaten.

6 January: Epiphany. Crosses are thrown into harbours on all coastlines. The young men who dive and retrieve them receive good luck for the coming year.

February–March: Carnival; masked bands of revellers take to the streets; harmless plastic hammers are sold to hit each other over the head.

Clean Monday: First day of Lent, 48 days before Easter, marked by kite-flying and outings to the countryside.

25 March: Greek Independence Day/Festival of the Annunciation; military parades.

Easter: The most important Orthodox holiday. Candlelit processions in each parish follow the flower-decked bier of Christ on Good Friday. The resurrection Mass at midnight on Holy Saturday is concluded with deafening fireworks and the relaying of the sacred flame from the officiating priests to the parishioners, who carefully take the candles home. On Sunday, lambs are roasted signifying the end of the Lenten fast. *Note that Orthodox Easter does not always fall on the same weekend as Roman Catholic and Protestant Easter.*

1 May: May Day or *Protomayiá*, marked by flower-gathering excursions to the country – and massive parades by the political Left.

24 June: Birthday of St John the Baptist. On the night before, bonfires are lit and the young leap over them.

15 August: Assumption Day. Processions and festivals across the country.

28 October: Óhi Day (*óhi* meaning 'no'), commemorating Greek defiance of the Italian invasion of 1940. Traffic comes to a halt.

November: Athens Marathon, commemorates arrival of the news of the defeat of the Persians.

December: Carols are sung door-to-door on the evenings of the twelve days of Christmas. On New Year's Eve, adults play cards for money, and a cake (the *vassilópita*) is baked with a coin hidden inside – good luck for whoever gets that slice on New Year's Day.

EATING OUT

The staples of Greek cuisine are local, seasonal ingredients at their peak of flavour and freshness, served raw, or cooked in the simplest fashions – on a grill, flash-fried, or slow-baked. Greeks have relied for centuries on staples like olive oil, wild herbs, seafood and lamb or goat's meat, along with an abundance of fresh vegetables, fruit, pulses and nuts, washed down with local wine. The traditional Greek diet is one of the healthiest in the world, and prices in all but the most luxurious establishments offer excellent value.

You will find numerous places to eat traditional Greek fare across Athens, but, like most other European capitals, it increasingly offers a range of exotic cuisines as well, in particular Italian and Asian. Greeks love to eat out, and new restaurant openings are intently reviewed in the local press. Both Greek and foreign-cuisine restaurants are listed in the Listings section *(see pages 136–42)*, but for those who want to discover Greek cuisine, the following information will help you to get the most from your menu.

WHERE TO EAT

In Greece you will find a range of eating establishments, each type specialising in certain dishes, and many are still family-run. The *ouzerí* purveys not just the famous aniseed-flavoured alcoholic drink, but also the *mezédes* (appetisers) that complement it – *oúzo* is never drunk on an empty stomach. Octopus or a platter of small fried fish are the traditional accompaniment, but there are also various other hot and cold vegetable and meat dishes to choose from.

The *psistaría* offers charcoal-grilled meats, plus a limited selection of salads and *mezédes*. The *tavérna* is a more elab-

Dining al fresco in Pláka

orate eatery, offering the pre-cooked, steam-tray dishes known as *mageireftá*, as well as a few grills and bulk wine. Restaurants *(estiatória)* and *inomageiría* (wine-and-food canteens) overlap considerably with tavernas, though they are less likely to have grilled items.

For sticky cakes, retire after your meal to a *zaharoplastío* – pastry or sweet shop – or a *galaktopolío*, which emphasises yoghurt, puddings and other milk-based dishes.

The *kafenío* is the Greek coffee shop, traditionally the domain of men only, and still so in the countryside and Greek island villages. Usually plainly decorated, they are the venues for political debate and serious backgammon and card games. Only drinks – including alcoholic and soft – are served.

Meal Times

Lunch is eaten between 2.30 and 4pm. Traditionally the meal would be followed by a siesta before work began again at

5.30pm, but this is fast changing in the capital. Dinner is eaten late – usually after 10pm, though many establishments will take last orders as late as 1am. If you want to eat early, some tavernas begin their evening service at around 7pm, but most don't open until 8pm. You will have your choice of table at this hour, but the atmosphere is definitely better later. Sunday evening and all day Monday are typical times of closure for those tavernas which do not operate every day.

WHAT TO EAT

You will usually be given an extensive menu (often in both Greek and English), which lists a vast array of dishes. Items currently available will have a price pencilled in beside them. However, your waiter is an even more reliable guide to what is available each day; the menu is most useful for checking

A traditional Greek salad *(horiátiki saláta)*

that the taverna is in your price range – especially for typically pricey items like meat or fish. It is also the rule to inspect the steam trays or chiller case to see what looks and smells enticing, and to order right there. This is a good way to familiarise yourself with the various Greek dishes.

All restaurants have a cover charge. This includes a serving of bread and usually costs no more than €1–2 per person.

Appetisers

Carefully selected, appetisers can constitute a full meal. *Mezédes* shared by the whole table are a fun and relaxing way to eat – you have as little or as much as you want and keep ordering until you have had your fill. *Ouzerís* in particular have no qualms about taking orders for '*mezédes* only' meals, bringing your choices out on a *dískos* or tray – though there is an optional round of hot mains-made-to-order.

The most common appetisers are *tzatzíki*, a yoghurt dip flavoured with garlic, cucumber and mint; *dolmádes*, vine leaves stuffed with rice and vegetables – sometimes mince – which can be served hot (with *avgolémono* sauce, made of eggs and lemon) or cold (with yoghurt); olives; *taramosaláta*, cod-roe paste blended with breadcrumbs, olive oil and lemon juice; *gígandes*, large beans in tomato sauce; *kalamári*, deep-fried squid; *mavromátika*, black-eyed peas; *tyrokafterí*, a spicy cheese dip; and *hórta*, boiled wild greens. *Saganáki* is yellow cheese coated in breadcrumbs and then fried, while *féta psití* is feta cheese wrapped in foil with garlic and herbs – often spicy ones – and baked.

Greek salad or *horiátiki saláta* (usually translated as 'village salad') of tomato, cucumber, onion, green peppers and olives topped with feta cheese, can be a meal in itself or can accompany any other dish. Cruets of olive oil and wine vinegar are found with other condiments on the table; add vinegar to the salad first, followed by oil.

Fish

Athens' proximity to the sea means that fresh fish *(psári)* is readily available, and throughout Attica you will find excellent seafood restaurants. The day's catch is displayed on ice inside a chiller case for you to make your choice, which will be weighed before cooking – but check the price first as seafood is priced by the kilo and is always a relatively expensive option. If the seafood is frozen or farmed (likely from June to October), this must by law be stated on the menu.

Larger fish is usually grilled and smaller fish fried; all are served with fresh lemon and *ladolémono* (olive oil with lemon juice). Most common species are *barboúni* (red mullet), *xifías* (swordfish), *tsipoúra* (gilt-head bream) and *fangrí* (bream). *Marídes* (picarel), *gávros* (anchovy) and *sardélles* (sardines) are served crisp-fried. For the ultimate luxury, order grilled *astakós* (spiny lobster). If you like seafood stewed, try *ktapódi krasáto*, octopus in red wine and tomato sauce; or *garídes* (prawns) in a cheese sauce *(saganáki)*. Fish soup, *psarósoupa*, is a standard on many seafood restaurant menus.

Fruit platters

Taverna favourites for fruit platters after meals vary according to season and include watermelon or Persian melon in summer; grapes in autumn; sliced apples with cinnamon or pears in winter; and citrus fruit or strawberries in early spring. Greece imports very little tropical fruit and just a few temperate fruits from Italy or Spain, so this is pretty much the repertoire.

Meat

Meaty snacks to take away include *gýros* (thin slices of pork cut from a vertical skewer and served with tomatoes, *tzatzíki* and lettuce in pitta bread), or *souvláki* (chunks of meat cooked on a skewer). Sit-down barbecued dishes include stuffed pork, sides of lamb or whole chickens, all cooked to a melting perfection. If you want a basic pork or veal cutlet, ask for *brizóla*; lamb or goat chops are called *païdákia*. Slow-cooked oven dishes and stews include *kokinistó* or *stifádo*, braised meat – such as rabbit – with baby onions.

Greece's most famous dish is probably *moussakás*, made with successive layers of potatoes, aubergine and minced beef topped with a generous layer of béchamel sauce. *Pastítsio* is another layered dish of macaroni, meat and cheese sauce, while *giouvétsi* is any meat stewed with lozenge-shaped pasta called *kritharáki*.

Two for the pot

For those who want a hot meatless dish, *gemistá* are tomatoes, aubergine or peppers stuffed with a delicious rice and vegetable mixture; alternatively, *melitsánes imám* is a rich dish of aubergine stuffed with tomato, garlic and oil.

Cheeses

Greek cheeses are made from cow's, ewe's or goat's milk, or often blends of two milks in varying proportions. The best-known cheese is *féta*, popping up in every Greek salad or served alone. *Graviéra* is the most common hard cheese, varying in sharpness; there are also many sweet soft cheeses such as *manoúri* and *anthótyro*.

Dessert

Most tavernas bring a plate of seasonal fresh fruit or semolina halva as a finale to your meal; for something more substantial, the *zaharoplastío* (sticky-cake shop) dishes out some of the more enduring legacies of the Ottomans, who introduced a number of incredibly decadent sweets including *baklavás*, layers of honey-soaked flaky pastry with walnuts; *kataïfi*, 'shredded wheat' filled with chopped almonds and honey; *galaktoboúreko*, custard pie; or *ravaní*, honey-soaked sponge cake. If you prefer dairy desserts, try yoghurt topped with local honey or fruit, or *ryzógalo*, cold rice pudding.

A splendid bottle of oúzo in the shape of a Greek temple

WHAT TO DRINK

Wine-making has a pedigree in Greece going back at least three millennia; modern production is centred in the regions of Macedonia, Thessaly, and the Peloponnese and on the islands of Crete, Rhodes, Kefalloniá, Santorini, Límnos and Sámos. In recent years, modern oenological methods have been introduced, improving the quality of bottled wines. Vintners to ask for include Tselepos, Ktima Papaïoannou, Tsantali, Spyropoulos, Lazaridi and Skouras.

The classic liquorice-flavoured Greek drink *oúzo* is taken as an aperitif with ice and water; a compound in the anise flavouring makes the mix turn harmlessly cloudy. The most popular brands come from the island of Lésvos. *Tsípouro* is a north mainland variant of this grape-mash distilled spirit, minus the anise. Another strong distilled spirit is *tsikoudhiá* which originates from Crete, though most Cretans refer to it by its Turkish name, *raki*.

There are nearly a dozen brands of beer produced in Greece, as well as imports. Foreign brands made under licence include Amstel, Kaiser and Heineken; local labels are Alfa (reckoned the best), Mythos, Fix, Pils Hellas and Vergina. Athens has its very own microbrewery called Craft, on Alexándras Avenue, which makes both light and dark beer; tours of the brewery are also available.

For a digestif, Greek-produced brandy is sweeter than French cognac. Metaxa is the most popular brand, sold (in ascending order of strength) in 3-, 5- and 7-star grades.

Bulk Wine and Retsína

Most tavernas offer house wine in bulk – ask *for hýma or varelísio* – which is generally much cheaper than bottled varieties. It is offered in full, half or quarter-litre measures, served either in pink or orange 'monkey cups' or glass flagons. This basic, rustic-style wine – whether red, white or rosé – will be served young and cool (cold in the case of white), though quality varies considerably; if in doubt, order a quarter-litre to start with as a test. Such wine is either *aretsínato* (unresined) or *retsína* (flavoured with pine resin). *Retsína* has been around since ancient times, when Greeks accidentally discovered the preservative properties of treating wine in this way. It complements the olive-oil base of oven-cooked dishes perfectly, but can be an acquired taste and should be served well chilled. The best *retsína* traditionally came from the Mesógeia district of Attica, but nowadays there are good brands of bottled *retsínas* such as Malamatina, Georgiadi and Liokri.

Cocktail, wine or beer?

Non-alcoholic Drinks

Hot coffee is made *ellínikós* or 'Greek' style (generic Middle Eastern style), freshly brewed in individual copper pots and served in small cups. It will automatically arrive *glykó* (very sweet) unless you order *métrio* (medium) or *skéto* (without sugar), but don't drink to the bottom as that's where all the grounds settle. Instant coffee (called 'Nes' irrespective of brand) has made big inroads in Greece; more appetising are the iced *kafés frappé* whipped up in a blender – especially refreshing on a summer's day – and very Greek despite the Italian-sounding name. Most cafés serve Italian-style espresso and cappuccino – though expect to pay Italian prices – and for fans of milky Seattle coffee, Starbucks can be found in Athens at various central locations.

Soft drinks come in all the usual varieties, and bottled *(emfialoméno)* Greek mineral water is available everywhere. Among the many brands, the best are Avra, Korpi and Zaros.

To Help you Order…

Could we have a table?	**Boroúme na éhoume éna trapézi?**
We would like to order…	**Thélume na parangílume…**
I'd like a/an/some…	**Tha íthela…**
A litre/half litre…	**Éna kiló/misókilo…**
I'm a vegetarian	**Íme hortofághos**
The bill, please…	**To logharyazmo parakaló…**

napkin	**hartopetséta**	fruit	**froúta**
cutlery	**maheropiroúnia**	garlic	**skórdo**
glass	**potíri**	goat	**katsíki**
one	**éna/mia**	greens	**hórta**
two	**dhýo**	honey	**méli**
three	**tris/tría**	lamb	**arní**
four	**téssera**	meat	**kréas**
fried	**tighanitó**	meatballs	**keftédhes**
roasted or grilled	**psitó**	milk	**gála**
		octopus	**ktapódi**
aubergine	**melitsána**	olives	**elyés**
beef	**moskhári**	pepper	**pipéri**
beer	**býra**	pork	**hirinó**
bread	**psomí**	prawns	**garídes**
butter	**voútiro**	salt	**aláti**
chicken	**kotópoulo**	sugar	**záhari**
chickpeas	**revíythia**	tomatoes	**dómates**
egg	**avgó**	water	**neró**
fish	**psári**	wine	**krasí**

Useful Expressions

Kalí órexi	Bon appétit
Kalí synnéhia	Good continuation (to the next course)
Yiámas	Cheers (as a toast)

HANDY TRAVEL TIPS

An A–Z Summary of Practical Information

A

ACCOMMODATION (see also YOUTH HOSTELS, and the list of
RECOMMENDED HOTELS on pages 128–35)

Hotels. For years, hotels have been classified in six categories –
Luxury, A, B, C, D and E – but since 2003 there has been a (largely ignored) attempt to replace this system with stars, from five down
to none. Room rates for all categories other than luxury are controlled by the Greek government. Categories are determined by the
common facilities at the hotel, not by the quality of the rooms. Thus,
a three-star/B-class hotel room may be just as comfortable as a five-
star/luxury hotel room, but will not have facilities such as a conference room, hairdresser, swimming pool or multiple restaurants.
All two-star/C-class hotels are en suite, clean and reasonably fur-
nished, and should provide breakfast. One-star/D-class hotels must
be en suite but will usually have little else on offer; no-star/E-class
are just about extinct in Athens.

Since a pre-Olympic Games overhaul of most Athens hotels, very
little remains in the city that could be called budget accommodation, at least of the savoury variety – you need to reckon on paying
at least €70 for a double room, which figure should include municipal tax and VAT. Savvy travellers have learned that Athens is at
its most pleasant in May–June and September–October, and these
are now reckoned peak seasons by most hoteliers; it can be easier
to secure a vacancy during July and August, but you should book
well ahead throughout the year to avoid disappointment. Reservations of less than three nights may attract a surcharge.

I'd like a single/double room	**Tha íthela éna monó/dipló domátio**
with bath/shower	**me bánio/dous**
What's the rate per night?	**Piá íne i timí giá mía níkta?**

AIRPORT

The **Elefthérios Venizélos airport** serving Athens is 27km (18 miles) from Sýntagma Square in the heart of the city. The airport **express bus** X95 (24 hours) will take you directly to Sýntagma Square in just over an hour if traffic is light (it can take almost two hours in heavy traffic); departures are every quarter-hour during the day, half-hourly between 11pm and 6am. At peak traffic times, and with light luggage, you might consider using the X94 bus which stops at the Ethnikí Ámyna metro station and continuing your journey into town from there, but this works out slightly more expensive (if quicker) than using the infrequent (half-hourly) **light-rail/metro** combination which has its own airport station. If you're headed out straight to the islands, or a beach suburb, it makes most sense to use the X96 express bus, which links the airport up to three times hourly with Karaïskáki Square in Piraeus via Vári, Voúla and Glyfáda.

The fare for all express buses is €3.20 and the ticket is only valid for a single journey into town, without using the metro. Buy your ticket at the kiosk outside the arrivals hall and validate it on the machine as you board the bus. The light-rail/metro combined ticket (you don't have to change cars) costs €6, or €5 each for groups of two or more.

A **taxi** will take just about the same time as the X95 bus and will cost roughly €20–30 from the airport to Sýntagma Square.

B

BUDGETING FOR YOUR TRIP

These are some rough estimates for your main expenses:
Scheduled flight from London: £140–£240 depending on season.
Scheduled flight from New York: $600–$1100 depending on season.
Hotel room in mid-range hotel in high season: €70–€130 per night.
Meal in mid-range taverna with house wine (per person): €15–€20.
Weekly car rental for a small car in high season: €320 unlimited mileage with a small local chain, €440 with a major international

chain. In low season this range becomes €190–€385. Especially if you want to pick up your car at the airport, it's worth pre-booking a car online before your journey.

Metro: €0.70–0.80 for a single ticket and €3 for a 24-hour ticket.

Museum and archaeological site entrance fees: €2–€12.

Beach entrance fee at some spots along the coast: about €5.

One-way ferry ticket to Égina: €9; to Póros: €15.

One-way hydrofoil/catamaran ticket to Égina: €12; to Póros: €25; to Ýdra: €28.

C

CAR HIRE (see also DRIVING)

Athens is a very congested city with a critical (and expensive) parking situation; the main tourist attractions are concentrated in such a small area that it makes little sense to hire a car. Using public transport will limit the amount of walking you do, and taxis are plentiful and cheap.

If you want to visit some islands, it is easier to take the metro to Piraeus, which terminates just across from the main harbour area – and of course cars are not carried on hydrofoils or catamarans, which serve all the Saronic Gulf islands. However, if you intend to spend a few days touring the Argolid or heading for Delphi, a car would definitely be an asset.

Those intending to hire a car should carry an international driver's licence if from the US, Canada or Australia (national licences alone will *not* be valid); alternatively all European Economic Area national driver's licences are accepted, provided that they have been held for one full year and the driver is over 21 years of age (sometimes 23 years for certain agencies). You will also need a credit or debit card to avoid fronting a large cash deposit.

Many brochure rates can seem attractive because they do not include personal insurance, collision damage waiver (CDW) or VAT at 19 percent. Most agencies have a waiver excess of between €400 and €600 – the amount you're responsible for if you smash a vehicle, even with CDW coverage. It is strongly suggested you purchase extra cover (often called Super CDW or Liability Waiver Surcharge) to reduce this risk to zero.

You will find all the major international chains represented in the arrivals concourse of the airport. In central Athens, almost all rental companies have offices at the very beginning of Syngroú Avenue in Makrigiánni district, and comparison shopping for quotes a day or so before you need a car can be very productive. Some smaller but reputable agencies to try include:

Autorent, Syngroú 11, tel: 210 92 32 514, www.autorent.gr
Avance, Syngroú 40–42, tel: 210 92 40 107, www.avance.gr
Bazaar, Syngroú 27, tel: 210 92 28 768, www.bazaarrac.gr
Budget, Syngroú 8, tel: 210 92 14 771, www.drivebudget.com
Kosmos, Syngroú 9, tel: 210 92 34 695, www.kosmos-carrental.com
Reliable, Syngroú 3, tel: 210 92 49 000, www.reliable.gr
Thrifty, Syngroú 25, tel: 210 92 43 304, www.thriftygreece.gr

I'd like to rent a car (tomorrow) for three days/a week	**Tha íthela na nikiáso éna avtokínito (ávrio) giá tris méres/mía evdomáda**

CLIMATE

Athens has a surprising range of climatic conditions and temperatures throughout the year. Some summer days can feature dry, furnace-like heat. Many Athenians leave the city during this season, and if you can avoid it, don't visit between late June and mid-September. From early June until the end of September, the weather is hot during the day and warm in the evenings, with 12–15 hours of sunshine per day. Between early October and late April, the weather can be quite changeable, with occasional wet and windy days. Snow occasionally falls in winter, but rain is more common.

Average air temperatures:

	J	F	M	A	M	J	J	A	S	O	N	D
Max °C	12	12	16	19	25	32	44	38	29	23	20	15
Max °F	54	54	60	66	76	90	110	100	85	74	65	58
Min °C	2	7	8	11	16	19	23	23	19	16	11	8
Min °F	35	44	46	52	60	66	72	72	66	60	52	46

Average water temperatures (Piraeus):

	J	F	M	A	M	J	J	A	S	O	N	D
°C	14	14	13	15	18	22	25	25	24	22	18	16
°F	57	57	55	59	64	72	77	77	75	72	64	61

CLOTHING

From early June to late September, light summer clothing will be all you need – with perhaps a wrap for later in the evening. Natural fibres are most comfortable, especially in midsummer. Even though you are in a city, take precautions with your skin and always carry something to cover arms and legs to avoid sunburn. Hats, sunglasses and long, loose sleeves are a must in summer.

In spring and autumn, take extra layers in case of a cold spell. In winter, bring a heavy coat or waterproof jacket, and a pocket umbrella, as Athens can be cold and wet. You can still experience very pleasant days late or early in the year, so a layering system – ie a pullover/sweater plus a light shell jacket – as for spring or autumn works well.

If you intend to enter any of the churches in the city you must be suitably dressed. No shorts for either sex, and women must have shoulders covered.

It cannot be overemphasised that comfortable, practical footwear is needed for touring the archaeological sites. Marble steps and walkways are worn slippery with age; other surfaces are uneven, which can result in twisted ankles.

If you intend to head out to the theatre or an upmarket restaurant, then take a dressier ensemble with you, though for most tavernas casual dress is quite acceptable.

COMPLAINTS (see also POLICE)

If you have a complaint, you should first take it up with the management of the establishment concerned. If, however, you get no satisfaction then you can approach the Tourist Police (tel: 171; offices on Veïkoú near corner Anastasíou Zínni, Koukáki district) whose English-speaking officers are specifically trained to deal with visitors who have problems – anything from petty theft to lost passports and complaints about taxi drivers, shopkeepers, tour guides and the like.

CRIME AND SAFETY (see also POLICE)

Central Athens is generally a safe place to visit with no inherent threats to visitors; however, just as in many large cities, petty crime (pickpocketing on buses and the old metro line in particular) and car break-ins (especially in Psyrrí and Exárhia) can be a problem so it pays to take some basic precautions.

• Never carry large amounts of cash.
• Leave all valuables in the hotel safe.
• Always walk in well-lit streets at night.
• Do not leave anything visible in vehicles.
• Always use official taxis – yellow ones with meters and illuminated roof signs.
• Don't let your attention be distracted from any of your bags.

It is always a good idea to have photocopies of any important paperwork and make a note of ticket numbers, passport number and traveller's cheque numbers just in case you do find yourself the victim of crime.

CUSTOMS AND ENTRY REQUIREMENTS

EU citizens can enter Greece for an unlimited length of time. British citizens must have a valid passport; citizens of Ireland can enter with a valid identity card or passport.

Citizens of the USA, Canada, Australia and New Zealand can stay in Greece for a total of 90 days cumulative in any period of 180 days upon production of a valid passport. South African citizens can stay for up to two months on production of a valid passport. No advance visas are needed for these stays, but extensions of the basic tourist stamp are almost impossible to obtain – you must leave the Schengen Zone for at least 90 days before re-entry. The Schengen Zone is the EU as it was before May 2004, minus Britain and Ireland, plus Norway and Iceland.

Greece has strict regulations about the import of drugs. All the obvious ones are illegal, but some seemingly beneficial drugs such as codeine and tranquillisers are also banned. Medicines prescribed by a doctor for personal use are permitted, so if you take any drug on medical advice then make sure you always carry enough for your needs during the entire stay and keep it in its original container.

The Greek authorities are understandably concerned about the loss of antiquities and national treasures, with many court cases pending overseas to secure the return of items illegally purchased or otherwise obtained by museums and galleries. Therefore, if you intend to buy an old piece, be it an icon or some statuary, always use a reputable dealer and make sure you keep your receipts. Genuine antiquities will need an export permit, in the absence of which you will be treated as a smuggler.

For citizens of non-EU countries, allowances for goods bought duty-free to be carried into Greece are as follows:

200 cigarettes or 50 cigars or 250g of tobacco
1 litre of spirits or 4 litres of wine
250ml of cologne or 50ml of perfume.

D

DRIVING

Road conditions. Athens' streets are often clogged with traffic, so on many occasions you can make better progress walking than driving. Drivers jostle for position, often running a changing (if not red) light, and seem to park wherever they please. Keep on the alert whether you are driving or walking.

The centre of Athens, the so-called *daktýlios*, has alternate-day driving. That is, vehicles with odd-numbered licence plates may go into the central zone on odd-numbered days, and even-numbered cars on even days – Monday to Friday 8am to 7pm. This includes rented vehicles with local Athens licence plates, though this provision tends not to be strictly enforced.

Most roads in the countryside have no verges or hard shoulders. This can cause problems if you need to slow down and leave the highway. If you get caught in a storm the road surface can become very slippery, especially in May when oily olive-tree blossom is dropping; most roads being banked wrongly at curves aggravates this problem.

Rules and regulations. Traffic drives on the right and passes on the left, usually yielding to vehicles from the right (from the left on roundabouts) – though this is not always followed by drivers, and accident rates are high. Transliteration schemes from Greek into Latin alphabet are not standardised, so you may find the same village is spelled different ways both on signage and on maps.

The speed limit on motorways is 120kmh (74mph), 90kmh (55mph)

Fill the tank, please.	**Óso pérnei, parakaló.**
Check the oil/tyres/battery.	**Na elénxete ta ládia/**
	ta lástiha/ti bataría.
My car has broken down.	**Épatha mía vlávi.**

on undivided roads, and in built-up areas 50kmh (30mph) unless otherwise stated, although many local drivers do not adhere to the regulations. Both speed limit and distance signs are in kilometres.

Seat belts are compulsory, as are crash helmets when riding a motorcycle or scooter. Drink-driving laws are strict, and checkpoints – particularly at weekends – conduct breath tests. Fines usually have to be paid at the nearest main police station.

Many districts have one-way systems to ease the flow of traffic around the narrow streets. Be aware that many scooter riders (and even some car drivers) do not obey these rules.

Road signs. Most road signs are the standard pictographs used across Europe. However, you may also meet some of these written signs:

ΑΠΑΓΟΡΕΥΕΤΑΙ Η ΑΝΑΜΟΝΗ	No waiting
ΑΠΑΓΟΡΕΥΕΤΑΙ Η ΕΙΣΟΔΟΣ	No entry
ΑΠΑΓΟΡΕΥΕΤΑΙ Η ΣΤΑΘΜΕΥΣΙΣ	No parking
ΔΙΑΒΑΣΙΣΠΕΖΩΝ	Pedestrian crossing
ΕΛΤΤΩΣΑΤΕ ΤΑΧΥΤΗΤΑ	Reduce speed
ΕΠΙΚΙΝΔΥΝΗ ΚΑΤΩΦΕΡΕΙΑ	Dangerous incline
ΕΡΓΑ ΕΠΙ ΤΗΣ ΟΔΟΥ	Road work in progress
ΚΙΝΔΥΝΟΣ	Caution
ΜΟΝΟΔΡΟΜΟΣ	One-way traffic
ΠΑΡΑΚΑΜΠΤΗΡΙΟΣ	Diversion (detour)
ΠΟΡΕΙΑ ΥΠΟΧΡΕΩΤΙ ΚΗ ΔΕΞΙΑ	Keep right
ΑΛΤ/ΣΤΟΠ	Stop

Fuel costs. At time of printing, petrol costs about €1.30 per litre depending on the grade; expect this figure to rise in line with increases elsewhere in the world. Petrol stations are open every day in season, between 6am and 8pm.

If you need help. If you have an accident or breakdown while on the road, put a red warning triangle some distance behind you to warn oncoming traffic. Always carry the telephone number of your rental office when you travel; it will be able to advise you if you have difficulties. If you have an accident involving another vehicle, do not admit fault or move either car until the local police come out and file a report; a copy will be given to you to present to the rental agency. Almost all agencies subscribe to one or other of the nationwide emergency roadside services (ELPA, Express Service, Ellas Service, Intersalonica); make sure you are given their respective nationwide numbers.

E

ELECTRICITY

The electric current throughout Greece is 220 volts/50 cycles. Electric plugs are of the European continental double round-pin type. Adapter plugs are available from electrical shops. Don't bring strictly 120-volt equipment – most modern hair dryers and shavers should have a dual voltage setting.

EMBASSIES AND CONSULATES

Australian Embassy: Soútsou 37 and Tsóha 24, 115 21 Athens: tel: 210 87 04 000, fax: 210 64 66 595.
British Embassy: Ploutárhou 1, 106 75 Athens, tel: 210 72 72 600, fax: 210 72 72 876.
Canadian Embassy: Ioánni Gennadíou 4, 115 21 Athens, tel: 210 72 73 400, fax: 210 72 73 480.

Irish Embassy: Vassiléos Konstandínou Avenue 7, 106 74 Athens, tel: 210 72 32 771, fax: 210 72 93 383.
New Zealand General Consulate: Kifissias Avenue 76, 153 23 Halándri, Athens, tel: 210 69 24 136, fax: 210 68 74 444.
South African Embassy: Kifissías Avenue 60, 151 25 Maroússi, tel: 210 61 06 645, fax: 210 61 06 640.
US Embassy: Vassilísis Sofías 91, 111 60 Athens, tel: 210 72 12 951, fax: 210 64 56 282.

EMERGENCIES

Police main number	Tel: **210 77 05 711**
Police emergency	Tel: **100**
Tourist Police	Tel: **171**
Fire	Tel: **199**
Ambulance	Tel: **166**

G

GAY AND LESBIAN TRAVELLERS

Greece is a very conservative country where traditional family re-lationships form the backbone of society. However, there is a nat-ural courtesy towards visitors and this combined with all the different types of international tourist makes Athens a good desti-nation for gay and lesbian travellers. There are a number of gay-friendly bars, cafés and restaurants in the districts of Makrigiánni (south of the Acropolis), Gázi (west of Kerameikos) and Exárhia (near Omónia).

GETTING THERE

By air. Olympic Airways (www.olympicairlines.com) is the nation-al carrier of Greece. It operates international flights to Athens from the following destinations: London (Heathrow and Gatwick), Man-chester, New York and Toronto.

From the UK, British Airways (UK tel: 0870 850 9850; Ireland tel: 1800 626 747; www.ba.com) also offers direct services from London Heathrow and London Gatwick; Aegean Airlines (Greece tel: 801 112 000; www.aegeanair.com) flies from London Stanstead; and easyJet (tel: 0870 000 000; www.easyjet.com) from Luton and London Gatwick. From Ireland, Aer Lingus (Ireland tel: 0818 365 000; www.aerlingus.com) flies daily from Dubin to Athens direct.

From North America, Delta (toll-free in the US: 001 800 22 11 212; www.delta.com) flies directly to Athens, from New York and Atlanta; Continental Airlines (US tel: 800 523 3273; www.continental.com) also fly New York–Athens direct. Otherwise you'll arrive indirectly via a European hub on such airlines as Lufthansa (www.lufthansa.com), KLM (www.klm.com), British Airways (www.ba.com) or Alitalia (www.alitalia.com). There are no direct flights from either Australia or New Zealand to Athens; the most likely advantageous providers of multi-stop flights include Gulf Air (www.gulfairco.com), Emirates (www.emirates.com), Singapore Airlines (www.singaporeair.com), Air New Zealand (www. airnewzealand.co.nz) and Qantas (www.qantas.com).

By car. The overland route to Greece from western Europe is not the quickest or easiest way to drive there. However, you can drive to the Italian ports of Venice, Ancona, Brindisi or Bari and take an overnight ferry to Igoumenítsa or Pátra on the Greek mainland. It is then a three-hour drive to Athens. The following companies currently offer trans-Adriatic service between Italy and Greece:

Agoudímos Lines	www.agoudimos-lines.com
ANEK	www.anek.gr
Maritime Way	www.maritimeway.com
Minoan Lines	www.minoan.gr
Superfast	www.superfast.com
Ventoúris	www.ventouris.gr

By rail. The train journey from the UK to Athens is expensive and takes 2–3 days. It is not possible to buy a return fare from the UK or Ireland to Greece in any case. Rail services from western European capitals can link with the ferries at Ancona or Brindisi for onward sailing to Pátra and rail transfer to Athens. It only really makes sense to arrive by train if you're on a longer tour of many European countries. In the UK, contact **Rail Europe** (tel: 0870 584 8848; www.raileurope. co.uk) for discounted youth rail fares and InterRail passes.

GUIDES AND TOURS

Only Greek Tourist Board-approved guides may conduct tours of archaeological sites. You will find official guides at the entrance to the Acropolis, or you can book a personal guide through any Greek National Tourist Organisation (EOT) office.

There is ample choice if you want to book a guided tour of Athens; however, walking tours are preferable to coach tours, which are likely to spend much of their time stalled in dense traffic. A coach tour is of most use for visiting Delphi, which is somewhat complicated to reach by public transport.

'Three-islands-in-one-day' cruises of the Saronic Gulf islands are eminently avoidable, allowing little time at each island. With a careful eye to hydrofoil or catamaran schedules (takeaway schedules usually available) you can construct your own itinerary taking in at least a couple of islands. Hotel reception desks are always happy to arrange land tours for you, with pick-up/drop-off at the hotel.

H

HEALTH AND MEDICAL CARE

In case of medical emergency, **dial 166** (Greek) for an ambulance or to find the nearest open hospital. Emergency treatment is given free at hospital casualty wards (ask for the *thálamo epigón peristatiká*), but this covers only immediate treatment. EU residents (including

UK and Irish nationals) will be able to get further free treatment, but must carry a European Health Insurance Card, obtainable on-line or by application to any post office. It is, however, always advisable to take out health/accident insurance to cover you for a health emergency while on a trip. Insurance will reimburse the cost of protracted treatment or repatriation should the need arise.

As mentioned in the Customs section *(see page 109)*, some medicines and prescription drugs that can be obtained normally in other countries are actually banned in Greece. For this reason, if you are taking any medication, take enough for your needs while on your trip and always keep it in its original packaging with original labels. There are no vaccination requirements for your trip to Greece.

For minor health problems, look for a pharmacy *(farmakío)*, signified by a green cross, where you will be able to obtain basic advice. Most pharmacists will speak some English.

If visiting Greece in the summer, always protect your skin against sunburn and keep yourself well hydrated. The tap water is safe to drink, though bottled spring water is universally available.

Where's the nearest (all-night) pharmacy?	**Pou íne to kondinótero (dianikterévon) farmakío?**
I need a doctor/dentist	**Chriázome éna giatró/odontogiatró**
an ambulance	**éna asthenofóro**
a hospital	**nosokomío**
I have...	**Écho...**
a headache	**ponokéfalo**
a fever	**piretós**
an upset stomach	**pónos stí kiliá**

HOLIDAYS

Official holidays, when most things will be shut, fall on the following dates:

1 January	New Year's Day *(Protohroniá)*
6 January	Epiphany
25 March	Greek Independence Day/Annunciation
1 May	May Day *(Protomagiá)*
15 August	Assumption of the Virgin
28 October	'No' or *'Ohi'* Day
25 December	Christmas Day
26 December	*Sýnaxis tis Panagías*
	(Gathering of the Virgin's Entourage)

The Greek Orthodox Easter is a moveable feast and its date is determined by the Julian calendar, which means that some years it coincides with the 'Western' (ie Catholic/Protestant) Easter, and other years it falls a week or two to either side of it (in fact anything up to four weeks). Moveable dates relative to Easter Sunday, all of them official holidays except Ascension Day, include the first day of Lent (Clean Monday; 48 days before Easter), Good Friday, Easter Monday, the Ascension (*Análipsi*; 39 days after Easter) and Pentecost (Whit Monday, *Ágion Pnévma*; 50 days after Easter).

L

LANGUAGE

Don't worry if you can't speak Greek. You will find that most people working anywhere near the tourist industry will have a basic English vocabulary and many speak English very well. Both the *Berlitz Greek Phrase Book and Dictionary* and *CD Pack* cover nearly all the situations you are likely to encounter in your travels.

In the centre of Athens most street signs are dually marked in Greek and Latin alphabets, and lots of tourist information (including taverna menus) is given in (often idiosyncratic) English. The table below lists the Greek letters in their upper- and lower-case forms, followed by the closest individual or combined letters to which they correspond in English.

Α	α	a	as in b**a**r
Β		v	as in **v**eto
Γ	γ	g	as in **g**o (except before '*i*' and '*e*' sounds, when it's like the *y* in **y**es)
Δ	δ	d	like **th** in '**th**is'
Ε	ε	e	as in g**e**t
Ζ	ζ	z	as in English
Η	η	i	as in s**ki**
Θ	θ	th	as in **th**in
Ι	ι	i l	as in s**ki**
Κ	κ	k	as in English
Λ	λ	l	as in English
Μ	μ	m	as in English
Ν	ν	n	as in English
Ξ	ξ	x	as in b**ox**
Ο	ο	o	as in g**o**t
Π	π	p	as in English
Ρ	ρ	r	as in English
Σ	σ, ς	s	as in ki**ss**
Τ	τ	t	as in English
Υ	υ	y	as in *country*
Φ	φ	f	as in English
Χ	χ	ch	as in Scottish *loch*
Ψ	ψ	ps	as in *tipsy*
Ο/Ω	ω	o	as in t**oa**d
ΟΥ	ου	oo	as in *soup*

M

MAPS

The Greek Tourist Office produces an excellent folding street map to aid your exploration of central Athens and Piraeus.

MEDIA

Television. Most hotels of B-class and above will offer satellite TV with foreign-language television, including CNN and BBC WORLD/ News 24. As far as Greek TV is concerned, there are three state channels in Athens, ET1, ET3 and NET, and a range of private ones.

Radio. Athens International Radio at 104.4FM broadcasts in English much of the day, often transmitting the BBC World Service.

Press. Numerous English-language newspapers (US and UK), sometimes a day old, are available at newsstands in the city. The Paris-based *International Herald Tribune* appears daily and includes as a bonus the English-language version of top local paper *Kathimerini*. The *Athens News* is published every Friday and has plenty of events listings and a TV guide. The bi-monthly *Odyssey* magazine has interesting features and book reviews, plus social/political commentary.

MONEY

Currency. Greece uses the euro (abbreviated €), which consists of notes of 5, 10, 20, 50, 100, 200, 100 and 500 euros; each euro comprises 100 cents and coins are issued in denominations of 1, 2, 5, 10, 20, 50 cents plus 1 and 2 euros.

Currency exchange. Most banks exchange foreign notes and traveller's cheques; they charge a percentage commission for the service of between one and three percent, queues are long, and frankly it's not worth the hassle since cash machines are ubiquitous in Athens and Greece generally (see ATMs, below). You can also use commercial bureaux de change, which are found in all the tourist centres and often keep longer hours than the banks. Some of these advertise 'commission-free' transactions but this is usually offset by a poorer exchange rate.

Always bring proof of identity with you such as a passport.

Automatic teller machines (ATMs). Most banks operate cash machines (ATMs) which accept just about any type of overseas debit card; look for your card's logo above the machine and key in your usual PIN (personal identification number). Despite commissions levied by your home bank running to nearly 3 percent (except for some consumer-friendly entities), this is the quickest and most convenient way to get cash.

Credit cards. Many hotels, restaurants, car hire companies, airline or ferry agencies and shops accept credit cards. Some companies make an additional charge for credit-card payments in order to cover their extra costs. It is always advisable to confirm credit-card acceptance before you sign the hotel register or order in a restaurant, to avoid difficulties later – especially in cheaper establishments.

I want to change some pounds/dollars.	**Thélo na alláxo merikés líres/meriká dollária.**
How much commission do you take?	**Póso promythia pérnete?**
Can I pay with this credit card?	**Boró na plíróso me avtí tin pistotikí kárta?**

O

OPENING TIMES

Banks are open Mon–Thur 8am–2.30pm, Fri 8am–2pm.
Most shops open Mon–Fri 9am–2pm, also Tue, Thur and Fri 5.30–8.30pm and Sat 9am–2.30pm; however, tourist shops – in Pláka for instance – will stay open seven days a week from 9am–10.30pm.

Museums and archaeological sites have unstable hours; do not assume you can gain admission anywhere except Tue–Sun 9am–2.30pm. The last admission is usually 20 minutes before closing.

P

POLICE (see also COMPLAINTS & CRIME AND SAFETY)

Greece's police force is divided into three: the regular local police, the port police and the tourist police. Athens' municipal police force wears greenish-grey uniforms in summer and green uniforms in winter. For emergencies dial 100, otherwise tel: 210 77 05 711.

Tourist police (tel: 171; offices on Veïkoú near corner Anastasíou Zínni, Koukáki district); these officers can speak English and can act as interpreters should your case need to involve the local police.

Where's the nearest police station?	**Pou íne to kondinótero astinomikó tmíma?**

POST OFFICES

Post offices, indicated by blue signs with a yellow stylised Hermes-head logo, are open from 7.30am–2pm. Stamps can be bought here and at substations in stationery shops. Postboxes are yellow for ordinary post and red for express. Packages for non-EU countries should not be sealed until they have been checked by post office staff.

The most central post offices in Athens, with additional afternoon and Saturday hours, can be found at 100 Odós Eólou (near Omónia Square), and at the corner of Sýntagma and Mitropóleos.

Where's the (nearest) post office?	**Pou íne to kodinótero tachidromío?**
A stamp for this letter/postcard, please.	**Éna grammató simo giaftó to grámma/graftí tin kárta, parakaló.**
express/registered	**exprés/sistiméno**
airmail	**aeroporikós**

PUBLIC TRANSPORT

Metro. The Athens metro is clean, fast and glitch-free, and you will find it is the best way to travel around Athens. The old, pre-2001 metro (Line 1), called ISAP, runs from Piraeus to Kifissiá. Line 2 runs between Ágios Dimítrios and Ágios Andónios. Line 3 runs between Monastiráki and Doukíssis Plakendías, with two special cars per hour, clearly marked, continuing beyond to the airport. The metro does not operate between midnight and 5.30am.

A single ticket costs €0.70–0.80 and is valid for a single one-way journey on the metro only; there's also a 90-minute ticket for €1.20. A 24-hour ticket valid for all means of transport – buses, tram, metro – costs €3, while a weekly pass is good value at €10. Tickets are purchased at metro stations, either from coin-op machines or an attended window. Fines for fare-dodging are a stiff 40 times the amount of the single fare evaded; rules are complicated and changeable, so unwitting violations occur. The main hazards for newcomers are attempting to switch from airport bus to metro (not allowed on the same ticket) or forgetting to validate tickets.

Buses and trams. An extensive bus network connects many places that the metro doesn't reach. Regular city buses run from 5am–11.45pm roughly every 20 minutes per route. They can be crowded, so for short journeys it may be easier to walk or get a taxi. Tickets (€0.60) can be purchased individually or in bundles of 10 from news kiosks and special booths at both bus-route start-points. Augmenting the blue-and-white buses are electric trolley buses.

Bus numbers beginning with 0 operate in central Athens; those beginning with 1 operate in the southern coastal suburbs as far as Vougliaméni; 2 to the south-central suburbs; 3 and 4 to southeastern and central Attica; 5 to Kifissía and the northern suburbs; 6 and 7 to the northwest; 8 westwards towards Daphni; 9 towards Piraeus.

The 2004-inaugurated tramway (tickets €0.80) operates routes from Sýntagma down to Glyfáda and to Néo Fáliro, with a link between the latter two points; it runs until 1am Sunday to Thursday, and (funding permitting) all night on Friday and Saturday.

The Athens Transport Office (OASA) issues a free map showing metro, tram and bus routes. This can be obtained from metro stations or from the OASA office at Odós Metsóvou 15, near the National Archaeological Museum.

Taxis. Taxis are numerous and cheap (they are painted yellow and have the sign TAXI atop the vehicle and on the side). Meters are set at the start of each journey; the '1' indicates regular fare, '2' indicates the rate between midnight and 5am. Prices are posted at the taxi stand at the airport, and basic charges appear on a laminated sheet mounted on the dashboard. In the city you can hail taxis in the street, but extra-long or short distances may be unpopular with drivers. All hotels will call a taxi for you which will pick you up at the reception. Fare-fiddling is not unknown, so the following sample '1' charges are useful: short hop across the centre, €3–6; city centre to Piraeus, €12. Trips to or from air/seaports have a small surcharge, and luggage in the boot gets charged at a rate of about €0.50 per item. The minimum fare is €1.75, and phoning for a taxi also adds to the total.

Ferries, catamarans, hydrofoils. Daily services operate to all the nearby islands, from Piraeus to the Saronic Gulf islands and the Cyclades, and from Rafína to the Cyclades. For details contact Piraeus Port Authority (tel: 210 42 26 000–4) or Rafína Port Authority (tel: 229 40 22 300) – however, English is not guaranteed to be spoken. If you have internet access and are planning on visiting the Saronic Gulf islands during your stay, then check the Hellenic Seaways website at www.hellenicseaways.gr or one of the following operators:
Vasilópoulos Flying Dolphins (to Égina only); tel: 210 41 19 500
Ágios Nektários Éginas (ferry to Égina only); tel: 210 42 25 625
Euroseas (catamaran to Póros, Ídhra, Spétses) tel: 210 41 32 105;
www.euroseas.com.

R

RELIGION (see also HOLIDAYS)

The established religion of Greece is **Greek Orthodox**, the largest religious minority being the indigenous Muslims of Thrace who constitute less than 2 percent of the total population. Most Greek festivals have a religious basis, and saints' days are celebrated everywhere.

The most important holiday in the Greek Orthodox calendar is Easter, which usually occurs anything up to four weeks either side of the Catholic and Protestant Easter. It is advisable to find out the date of Easter before booking a spring holiday as services, shops and (especially) flights experience disruption at this time.

Other religions that have representation in the city include:
Church of England: St Paul's, Odós Filellinon 29
American Church: St Andrew's, Sina 66
Roman Catholic: St Denis, Panepistimíou 24.

T

TELEPHONES

The Telecommunications Organisation of Greece (**OTE**, known as *oh-tay*) is the basic provider of domestic and international communications, but the industry has been deregulated and private long-distance companies abound. All street-corner public telephones are card-operated; buy 100- or 500-unit cards from newsstands and kiosks, but use these only for local or short intercity calls. Most people now use prepaid calling cards (most cost €5) for ringing mobiles or overseas, at half to a third of OTE tariffs. These work, via an 807 access number, from any fixed private phone or call box (but not a mobile).

Most hotels of C class and above have direct-dial telephones in the rooms, but it is unwise to use them for anything other than brief local calls to land lines. Surcharges are at least triple the basic OTE rates; avoid them by either using pre-paid cards as described above, or using your credit card and a direct call centre.

All phone numbers in Greece have 10 digits; as in France, there are no area codes per se – you must dial all 10 digits even when within the same former 'area code' (now the prefix). Land lines begin with 2, mobiles with 6. The international code for Greece is 30. When dialling out of Greece, international country codes are all prefixed by 00.

Foreign mobile-phone owners will find themselves well catered for in terms of thorough coverage and roaming agreements with most overseas providers. The cost of roaming in Europe has fallen considerably, but if you're going to be staying longer than a week it may still be worth buying a local pay-as-you-go SIM card for about €20; if necessary, your phone can be unblocked for a small charge. North American users will have to bring a tri-band apparatus to use their phone.

TICKETS FOR EVENTS

There is no central ticketing organisation in the city. Each venue must be approached separately.

TIME ZONES

Greece operates two hours ahead of Britain (Greenwich Mean Time), and one hour ahead of European countries on Central European Time. Like Britain, Greek summertime means that clocks move one hour ahead on the last Sunday in March and one hour back on the last Sunday in October. For North America, the difference is 7 hours for Eastern Standard Time and 10 hours for Pacific Standard Time (plus or minus an hour during those periods affected by Daylight Saving).

New York	London	**Athens**	Sydney	Auckland
5am	10am	**noon**	7pm	9pm

TIPPING

Service is included in restaurant and bar bills although it is customary to leave any small change on the table, up to 10 percent of the bill. In the week before Easter and at Christmas restaurants add an extra 'bonus' to the bill for the waiters.

At hotels, unless service is included (check as many hotels add 12 percent to the price of the room), chambermaids should be left a tip of around €1 per day, and porters and doormen should be tipped up to €1.50, depending on services provided.

Taxi drivers are apt to round up to the nearest euro.

Attendants in toilets should be left around €0.50.

TOILETS

All the main tourist attractions have good public facilities. Public parks and squares also have them, sometimes subterranean. Most cafés will have facilities – these vary in cleanliness – but you should be a patron of the café to use them. Also be aware that in many establishments toilet paper is still disposed of in the bin, not the toilet bowl, due to narrow pipes and ancient plumbing.

Where are the toilets?   **Pou íne ta apohoritíra?**

TOURIST INFORMATION

The Ethnikós Organismós Tourismoú, popularly known as **EOT**, is known in English as the **Greek National Tourist Organisation**. It operates tourist information offices in several countries outside Greece as well as within the country.

The EOT information office in Athens is inconveniently situated out on Anastasíou Tsóha between Tsoútsou and Vassilísis Sofías (Mon–Fri 8.30am–2pm; tel: 210 33 10 392). For tourist information before you travel to Greece, visit their website at www.gnto.gr, or contact one of the following offices:

Australia and New Zealand 51–75 Pitt Street, Sydney, NSW, tel: (2) 92411663, fax: (2) 92352174, email: hto@tpg.com.au.
Canada 1170 Place du Frère André, Suite 300, Montréal, Quebec H3B 3C6, tel: (514) 871 1535, www.greektourism.com.
UK and Ireland 4 Conduit Street, London W1R 0DJ, tel: (020) 7734 7997, fax: (020) 7287 1869, www.gnto.co.uk.

Where's the tourist office?   **Pou íne to grafío tourismoú?**

US Olympic Tower, 645 Fifth Avenue, New York, NY 10022, tel: (212) 421-5777, fax: (212) 826-6940, www.greektourism.com.

W

WEBSITES

Websites for useful organisations have been included in other sections of this guide; however, the following general websites will help you to plan your trip to Athens:
www.athensguide.com
www.athensnews.gr
www.athenstourism.gr
www.culture.gr
www.ekathimerini.gr
www.gtp.gr

Y

YOUTH HOSTELS

The following are two of the better student hostels in Athens, but go to www.hostelsweb.com/cities/athens.html for an up-to-date listing:
Athens Backpackers, Makri 12, tel: 210 92 24 044.
Student and Traveller's Inn, Kydathinéon 16, tel: 210 32 44 808.

Recommended Hotels

The following recommendations cover the main central districts of Athens, plus the most popular excursion venues around the city, and offer hotels for all budgets. To make a telephone enquiry or booking from overseas, preface the telephone numbers with the international code 00 30 (011 30 from North America).

Prices fluctuate across the year, with a difference of as much as 40 percent between high and low seasons. Tax and service charges should be included in quoted rates, though breakfast (typically €5–12 per person) may not be – check. The prices indicated below are for a double room per night in high season.

€€€€€	over 200 euros
€€€€	150–200 euros
€€€	100–150 euros
€€	60–100 euros
€	below 60 euros

MAKRYGIANNI & VEIKOU

Acropolis Select €€€ *Falírou Street 37–39, 117 42 Athens, metro Acropolis, tel: 210 92 11 611, fax: 210 92 16 938, www.acropolisselect.gr.* A recently renovated hotel with helpful staff and a prime location. It has a pleasant if dark-toned lounge-bar, a plush breakfast area, off-street parking, and wi-fi access in rooms for an hourly fee, but no roof garden. Some rooms have Acropolis views. 72 rooms.

Art Gallery €€ *Erehthíou 5, 117 42 Athens, metro Syngroú-Fix, tel: 210 92 38 776, fax: 210 92 33 025, www.artgalleryhotel.gr.* This small pension-hotel, named after the artwork on the walls of the common areas, has a variety of nicely-furnished, parquet-floored rooms, with family-sized suites on the roof. Pleasant breakfast bar on the terrace with Acropolis views. 22 rooms.

Athenian Callirhóe €€€€ *Kallíróis 32, corner Petmezá, 117 43 Athens, metro Syngroú-Fix, tel: 210 92 15 353, fax: 210 92 15 342,* *www.tac.gr*. Athens' first boutique hotel offers designer-tweaked rooms, with glass partitions, leather and metal trim, and internet access. Facilities include conference halls, café, nightclub and a roof garden restaurant with Acropolis views during summer. 84 rooms.

Héra €€€€ *Falírou 9, 117 42 Athens, metro Acropolis, tel: 210 923 6682, www.herahotel.gr.* The *Héra* has perhaps the best roof garden in the area, with a heated bar-restaurant for all-year operation. Rooms are on the small side, so it's worth an extra supplement for the fifth-floor suites with bigger balconies. The dome-lit atrium-breakfast room, and friendly staff, are further assets. 38 rooms.

Heródion €€€€ *Rovértou Gálli 4, 117 42 Athens, metro Acropolis, tel: 210 92 36 832, fax: 210 92 11 650, www.herodion.gr.* The *Heródion* scores most points for its common areas: the café-restaurant with patio seating shaded by wild pistachios, and the roof garden with two Jacuzzi tubs and the Acropolis a stone's throw away. Functional but fair-sized rooms, some with Acropolis views. 90 rooms.

Marble House € *Alley off Anastasíou Zínni 35, 117 41 Athens, metro Syngroú-Fix, tel: 210 92 28 294 or 694 57 56 383, fax: 210 92 26 461, www.marblehouse.gr.* This welcoming, family-run pension has an enviably quiet location. Upstairs rooms are simple but tidy, with balconies. baths, fridges and air con, but no phones. Great value – book well in advance. 16 rooms. Credit cards for deposit only.

PLAKA

Acropolis House €€ *Kódrou 6–8, 105 57 Athens, metro Sýntagma, tel: 210 32 22 344, fax: 210 32 44 143, www.acropolishouse. gr.* The first neoclassical mansion in Athens to be converted into a pension. The building's listed status prevents its creaky rooms getting a facelift, though for the academic clientele that's part of the charm. Some rooms are en suite and most have high ceilings (some with murals). Communal fridge and breakfast room. 19 rooms. Cash only.

Electra Palace €€€€€ *Navárhou Nikodímou 18–20 105 57 Athens, tel: 210 33 70 000, fax: 210 32 41 875, www.electrahotels.gr.* The only real luxury outfit in Pláka, the neoclassical *Electra Palace* is an oasis, with a small pool and pleasant spa in the basement, and a lawn garden just outside. Luxury suites have dark wood floors, oriental rugs and Jacuzzis; all rooms have high speed internet connection. A new wing with a rooftop pool has recently been added. 155 rooms.

Hermés €€€ *Apóllonos 19, 105 57 Athens, metro Sýntagma, tel: 210 32 35 514, fax: 210 32 22 412, www.hermeshotel.gr.* Part of a family-run chain, the *Hermés* has a breakfast room on the mezzanine, decorated with manager Dorína Stathopoúlou's professional photographs. The street-level lounge-bar is naturally lit by a light well. Front-facing rooms are smaller but have balconies, and all rooms have marble baths. 45 rooms.

Phaédra € *Herefóntos 16, corner Adrianoú, 105 58 Athens, metro Acropolis, tel: 210 32 38 461, fax: 210 32 27 795.* Rescued from dilapidation before the Olympics, the *Phaédra* now offers the best budget value in Pláka. Not all rooms are en suite, but some have balconies looking onto the square with its Byzantine church. Breakfast is served in a pleasant ground-floor salon. 21 rooms. Cash only.

Pláka €€€ *Kapnikaréas 7, corner Mitropóleos, 105 56 Athens, metro Monastiráki, tel: 210 32 22 096, fax: 210 32 22 412, www.plaka hotel.gr.* Part of the same group as the *Hermés*, the *Pláka* shares many of its characteristics. All rooms have fridges, internet access and balconies, half facing the Acropolis. Good roof garden and cheerful mezzanine breakfast salon, plus a lounge on each floor. 67 rooms.

MONASTIRAKI AND PSYRRI

Arion €€€ *Agíou Dimitríou 18, 105 54 Athens, metro Monastiráki, tel: 210 32 40 415, www.arionhotel.gr.* This hotel in the heart of Pysrrí – has good-sized Japanese accented rooms with lattice closet doors, modular headboards, square light fittings, but no balconies (though there is a common roof terrace). Quiet despite its proximity to the area's *ouzerís* and bars. 51 rooms.

Attalos €€ *Athinás 29, 105 54 Athens, metro Monastiráki, tel: 210 32 12 801, fax: 210 32 43 124, www.attalos.gr.* This friendly, centrally located hotel is good value and retains many of its period features, but the rooms themselves – about half with balconies – have modern furnishings, double glazing against street noise and parquet floors. Facilities include free use of a wi-fi hotspot and a very popular roof terrace operating from 6.30pm onwards. 80 rooms.

Carolina €€ *Kolokotróni 55, 105 60 Athens, metro Panepistimíou or Monastiráki, tel: 210 32 43 551, fax: 210 3243 550, www.hotel carolina.gr.* The *Carolina* is back in business after some years of closure. The best – if potentially hottest – rooms are the fifth-floor 'retirées' up on the roof garden; all others have balconies, and the rear-facing units have limited Acropolis views. 31 rooms.

Cecil €€ *Athinás 39, 105 54 Athens, tel: 210 32 17 079, fax: 210 32 18 005, www.cecil.gr.* This well-restored 1850s vintage mansion has some great period features such as its interwar iron-cage elevator. For preservation reasons, the rooms have no balconies – unless you count the ornamental ones out front – but they offer parquet floors, iron bedsteads, double glazing, pastel colours and retiled baths. 40 rooms.

OMONIA

Art Athens €€ *Márni 27, 104 32 Athens, metro Omónia, tel: 210 52 40 501, fax: 210 52 43 384, www.arthotelathens.gr.* Set in an interwar Art Nouveau/neoclassical building, this hotel offers one-of-a-kind rooms. Bathrooms are also unique, most with chrome sinks. Common areas include an events hall and stunning reception atrium with a circular light well. Pricing reflects the less desirable area, though you are close to the Archaeological Museum. 30 rooms.

Baby Grand €€€€ *Athinas 65, 105 51 Athens, metro Omónia, tel: 210 32 50 900, fax: 210 32 50 920, www.classicalhotels.com.* Once a fairly pleasant but rather anonymous hotel, the Baby Grand today is one of the most stylish boutique hotels in Athens. It has a great sense of fun about it, from the reception desks which are in fact made from

Mini Cooper cars, to the 'graffiti' rooms, decorated by local artists. The Spiderman room is often booked ahead. There's also a small spa, an excellent restaurant, and the first champagne bar in Athens.

Fresh €€€€ *Sofokléous 26, corner Klisthénous, 105 52 Athens, metro Omónia, tel: 210 52 48 511, fax: 210 52 48 517, www.freshhotel.gr.* You will either love or hate this startling 'design' hotel, with its lollipop colour scheme of panels everywhere from reception to the balconies. Chrome, leather and glass abound, but there is also plenty of oak and walnut. Modern room features include bedside remote control of windows and plasma TV. The rooftop pool-and-bar is a big hit and the six superior rooms have private Zen rock gardens. 133 rooms.

SYNTAGMA

Grande Bretagne €€€€€ *Platía Syntágmatos, metro Sýntagma, tel: 210 33 30 000, fax: 210 32 28 034, www.grandebretagne.gr.* Perhaps the most famous hotel in Athens, oozing history and class, the *Grande Bretagne* on Sýntagma Square dates from 1846. A recent renovation restored every period detail to its *belle époque* glory. 'Deluxe' doubles are like junior suites elsewhere. Sumptuous common areas include a landscaped pool garden, a ballroom, plus a basement spa with a palm court, and large pool, hamam and sauna. 321 rooms.

King George Palace €€€€€ *Platía Syntágmatos, metro Sýntagma, tel: 210 32 22 210, fax: 210 32 50 504, www.classicalhotels.gr.* The *King George Palace* is a more intimate, scaled-down version of the *Grande Bretagne*. It has the same Second Empire furnishings, which jar a bit with the flat-screen TVs, recessed lighting and sound systems. Bathrooms are palatial, with marble trim. Actively pitched at a business clientele, with a gym and spa. 110 rooms and suites.

KOLONAKI

St George Lycabettus €€€€ *Kleoménous 2, 106 75 Athens, metro Evangelismós, tel: 210 72 90 711, fax: 210 72 90 439, www.sglyca bettus.gr.* Recently renovated hotel at the foot of Mount Lykavittós (Lycabettus). Room décor varies from plush to minimalist; all have wi-fi access, and some have views over the city. Facilities include Jacuzzi, sauna, massage studio, gym and roof pool. 154 rooms.

Periscope €€€€–€€€€€ *Háritos 22, 106 75 Athens, metro Evangelismós, tel: 210 72 97 200, fax: 210 72 97 206, www.periscope.gr.* Slick hotel with arresting black-, white- and grey-toned rooms. Wall and ceiling art includes real-time projection of the skyline relayed by… a periscope! The higher in the building, the better the units, culminating in airy balconied suites, and a rooftop Jacuzzi. All units have wood floors, flat-screen TVs and CD/DVD players. 22 units.

AMBELOKIPI (PLATIA MAVILI)

Airotel Alexandros €€€ *Timoléontos Vássou 8, 115 21 Athens, metro Ambelókipi, tel: 210 64 30 464, fax: 210 64 41 084, www.airotel.gr.* Located on a little square behind a chapel, the *Airotel Alexandros* has comfortable accommodation in a slightly forbidding exterior. The high-ceilinged lounge is flanked by the brick-and-pastel-panelled restaurant; there are also three conference rooms. 96 rooms.

Androméda €€€€ *Timoléontos Vássou Street 22, 115 21 Athens, metro Ambelókipi, tel: 210 64 15 000, fax: 210 64 66 361, www.andromedaathens.gr.* One of the first boutique hotels in the city, with an African-themed lobby and Second-Empire décor in the first-floor restaurant and breakfast salon. Standard rooms lack balconies, but suites have them at both front and back; furnishings are a bit dated – the apartments are better. 21 rooms, 10 suites, 12 apartments.

ARGOLID PENINSULA

La Belle Hélène € *Main road, Mykínes 212 00 (Mycenae), tel: 27510 76225, fax: 27510 76179.* This 1862-built house retains its Victorian ambience – you can even sleep in the bed Heinrich Schliemann used during his excavations at Mycenae. Conservation rules mean bathrooms are not en suite, but the hospitality is excellent. The guestbook has signatures of the famous (eg Agatha Christie, Virginia Woolf) and infamous (assorted Nazi brass). 5 rooms. Cash only.

Candia House €€€€–€€€€€ *211 00 Kándia Iríon, tel: 27520 94060, fax: 27520 94480, www.candiahouse.gr.* A small luxury hotel owned by a delightful Athenian, who wanted to create a peaceful haven for her guests. On a sandy beach 17km (11 miles) southeast of Náfplio, it is ideally placed for touring the area. The individually designed suites have living rooms, kitchens and balconies. Facilities include a pool, gym and sauna. Open May–Oct. 10 suites.

Mariánna €€ *Potamianoú 9, 211 00 Náfplio, tel: 27520 24265, fax: 27520 99365, www.pensionmarianna.gr.* Restored and run by three hospitable brothers, this house-pension nestles against Akronafplía fortress's rocky walls, its patios planted with orange trees. Rooms, some with exposed masonry, are attractive and comfortable. Delicious home-made breakfasts are served on a raised terrace with fabulous views over the old town and the bay. 21 rooms.

SARONIC GULF ISLANDS

Bratséra €€€€ *180 40 Ýdra (Hydra), tel: 22980 53971, fax: 22980 53626.* The top accommodation on the island, this hotel occupies a former sponge factory, and the extensive common areas (including a conference room and Ýdra's only pool) double as a museum, with photos and artefacts. Rooms have flagstone floors and showers. Open mid-Mar–Oct. 23 rooms.

Brown €€ *Southern waterfront, past Panagítsa church, 180 10 Égina, tel: 22970 22271, www.hotelbrown.gr.* Égina town's top hotel, opposite the southerly beach, occupying a former sponge factory dating from 1886. The best and calmest units are the garden bungalows at the rear; there are also galleried family suites sleeping four.

Eginítiko Arhontikó €€ *corner Thomaïdhou and Ayíou Nikólaou, 180 10 Égina, tel: 22970 24156, fax: 22970 26716, www.aegini tikoarchontiko.gr.* A late 18th-century neoclassical mansion, now converted into a small hotel with well-appointed rooms. The *pièce de résistance* is the suite with painted ceilings. There is also a breakfast conservatory with coloured glass. 10 rooms. Cash only.

Ikonómou Mansion €€€€–€€€€€ *Kounoupítsa district, 400m from Dápia port, 180 50 Spétses town, tel: 22980 73400, fax: 22980 74074.* Spetses' premier restoration inn is part of an 1851-vintage property. The ground floor of the main house has six well-converted rooms with ample period features; a newer outbuilding hosts two luxury sea-view suites. Breakfast served by the pool. 8 units. Cash only.

Nissiá €€€€€ *Kounoupítsa district, 500m from Dápia port, 180 50 Spétses town, Spétses, tel: 22980 75000, fax: 22980 75012, www.nissia.gr.* Built on the grounds of an early 20th-century factory (of which only the Art-Nouveau façade remains), this luxury facility boasts a large pool. Units have fully equipped kitchens. 40 units.

Hotel Seven Brothers €€ *Póros town, tel: 22980 23412, fax: 22980 23413, www.7brothers.gr.* Situated at the corner of a fairly quiet little square just off the seafront, the *Seven Brothers* puts you at the heart of pretty Póros town. Open Apr–Oct. 16 rooms.

DELPHI AREA

Ganimede/Ganymídis €€ *Southwest market street, 330 52 Galaxídi, tel: 22650 41328, fax: 22650 42160, www.ganimede.gr.* This restored hotel in an historic port to the south of Delphi makes a relaxing base. There are six doubles in the old ship-captain's mansion and a family suite across the courtyard garden where a copious breakfast is served, featuring exquisite homemade pâtés and jams. 7 rooms.

Pan €€ *Pávlou ké Frederíkis 53, 330 54 Delfí, tel: 22650 82294, fax: 22650 83244.* Comfortable small hotel with fine views of the gulf. The *Artemis* annexe opposite has doubles equal in standard to the *Pan's* family quads but lacking the sea views. 21 rooms jointly.

Xenónas Generáli €€–€€€ *Eastern outskirts below clocktower, 320 04 Aráhova, www.generalis.gr.* The best accommodation in town: 13 unique, named rather than numbered rooms, most with fireplaces. The décor in some can be a bit precious, but the welcome is warm. In the basement, an indoor pool, spa, hamam and sauna are all popular with the après-ski set. 13 rooms.

Recommended Restaurants

Athens and its surroundings offer an astounding range of culinary opportunities. Follow the locals for the best cuisine, and you should not be disappointed. Many restaurants close in summer, or on Sundays.

Relatively few restaurants accept credit cards, and we state where this is the case, but it is always worth checking ahead. Few restaurants have no-smoking sections, so eating in the open air is often the only way to escape the smoke. Reservations are advisable if you plan to eat at one of the finer establishments, particularly at the weekend.

Most of the following recommendations lie within the city centre area close to public transport routes or a short taxi ride from central hotels. Prices indicated are for dinner per person without wine.

€€€€€	over 40 euros
€€€€	30–40 euros
€€€	20–30 euros
€€	15–20 euros
€	below 15 euros

EXARHIA

Bárba Giánnis € *Emmanouíl Benáki 94, metro Omónia, tel: 210 38 24 138.* One of the last surviving *inomagería* (wine-and-casserole-food kitchens), serving consistently good, if a bit stodgy, fare, such as *fáva*, *giouvarláki* (rice-and-meat rissoles in *avgolémono* sauce) or baked mackerel. Outdoor seating in summer. Open 11am–1.30am, closed Sun night and Aug. Cash only.

Fasóli €€ *Emmanouíl Benáki 45, metro Omónia, tel: 210 33 00 010.* Recently opened, with trendy utilitarian décor such as fairy lights. The food is solid Greek with creative twists: lentil salad, *biftéki* roulade, light pasta dishes, the usual starters and excellent value-for-money *fasóli*. The specials board is worth consulting. Closed Sun. Cash only.

O Pinaléon €€ *Mavromiháli 152, metro Ambelókipi, tel: 210 64 40 945.* This indoor taverna has acquired a cult following for its rich *mezédes* (offered on a *dískos*), mains such as smoked pork loin, own-brewed red wine, and *mastíha* (a Hiot drink) as a digestif. It is usually lively, with close-packed tables, so you are wise to book. Open late Sept–mid-May, supper only. Cash only.

KOLONAKI

L'Abreuvoir €€€€ *Xenokrátous 51, at Platía Dandé, metro Evangelismós,* tel: 210 72 29 106. Tucked away just behind the Gennadion Institute, this long-running French restaurant purveys a *carte* of three to four starters and mains per day, often including game. You can eat out under the trees on the plaza in fine weather.

Filíppou € *Xenokrátous 19, metro Evangelismós,* tel 210 72 16 390. This *estiatório*, founded in 1923, serves honest fare such as baked sardines and potatoes with dill, washed down with excellent bulk wine. Service is low-key but efficient; the dining room was recently redecorated, but has kept a pleasant retro air with proper table napery. Open noon–late except Sat eve, Sun and part of Aug. Cash only.

Kiku €€€€€ *Dimokrítou 12, metro Sýntagma,* tel: 210 36 47 033. Arguably the best Japanese cuisine in Athens, served in contemporary minimalist surroundings. The fare encompasses sushi, sashimi and tempura, plus udon noodles and yakisoba. Open supper only, Mon–Sat.

To Kioúpi € *Platía Kolonakioú 4, metro Sýntagma,* tel: 210 36 14 033. This classic basement *inomagerío*, with its original, attractive stone walls exposed, is an open secret among the locals. Favourite dishes include *gída vrastí* (stewed goat) and *gouronópoulo* (suckling pig). Closed Sun, Aug and after 7pm in summer. Cash only.

Il Postino €€€ *Grivéon 3, pedestrian lane off Skoufá, metro Panepistimíou,* tel: 210 36 41 414. A genuine *osteria* with an unpretentious menu, supervised by an Italian chef with an illustrious track record in Athens. Sit in the quiet cul-de-sac outside or in the basement with its old-photo décor and retro music. Open 1.30pm–late Mon–Sat.

MAKRYGIANNI/KOUKAKI

Amvrosía € *Márkou Drákou 3–5, metro Syngroú-Fix, tel: 210 92 20 281*. Of the many bars and restaurants on the pedestrianised street leading up from the metro entrance towards Filopáppou hill, *Amvrosía* is perhaps the best value for a meat feed. There is also a full range of starters, bulk wine and beer. Cash only.

Edódi €€€€€ *Veïkoú 80, metro Syngroú-Fix, tel: 210 92 13 013*. One of the city's best 'nouvelle' restaurants, an intimate, eight-table affair, on the upper floor of a neoclassical house. The international fusion menu changes regularly but is likely to include dishes such as duck in cherry sauce or smoked-goose carpaccio. Attentive staff; save room for the creative desserts. Open Mon–Sat, supper only; closed summer.

Mets €€€ *Markou Moussourou 14, metro Akrópoli (long walk), tel: 210 92 29 454*. This is a long-established local hang-out, a little out of the centre but worth it. It's both a jazz bar and a very casual restaurant, where people go to have a good time and relax, rather than a formal meal – but the food is reliably good. Open daily noon–2am.

MONASTIRAKI/PSYRRI/THISSIO

Café Avissinía €€€ *Kynéttou 72, metro Monastiráki, tel: 210 32 17 047, www.avissinia.gr*. After browsing the weekend flea market, there is no more atmospheric place to retire to than *Café Avissinía* for hearty, Macedonian-influenced food and a spot of bohemian entertainment courtesy of an accordionist and singer. Upstairs and outdoor tables are quieter. Open noon–late, closed Sun at 7pm, Mon & summer.

O Nikítas € *Agíon Anargýron 19, metro Monastiráki, tel 210 32 52 591*. Probably the oldest (1967-founded) taverna in Psyrrí, *O Nikítas* purveys a short but sweet menu, as well as daily specials like oven-baked cheese pie. Drink is confined to beer or ouzo, and there are no sweets. Nonetheless for good value you can't beat it, especially if seated outdoors under the trees on the pedestrian walkway by Agíon Anargýron church. Open noon–6pm Mon–Sat. Cash only.

To Stéki tou Ilía €€ *Eptahalkou 5, tel 210 34 58 052, and Thessaloníkis 7, tel 210 34 22 407, metro Thissío.* The two branches of this enterprise fill with locals who come for the house speciality: a big pile of grilled lamb chops. Starters are competent, service is quick, and barrelled wine is very reasonable. Book for a table outside, or sit indoors under the wine barrels. Open Mon–Sat supper only, Sun lunch, may close Mon outside of summer. Cash only.

Tavérna tou Psyrrí € *Eskhýlou 12, metro Monastiráki, tel: 210 32 14 923.* Trendy, overpriced eateries are ten a penny in Psyrrí; this is one of the few normal-priced traditional tavernas, and accordingly popular, so show up early. The menu is strong on fish and seafood; when ordering, bear in mind that portions are huge. There is a garden out back, and the inside is decorated with old photos and gravures of Athens. Service can be brusque. Open noon–1am. Cash only.

Thanássis € *Mitropóleos 69, tel: 210 32 44 705.* Three hotly competing *souvlatzídika* (souvlaki stalls) cluster here where Mitropóleos meets Platía Monastirakíou, but the queues make it obvious which is the best. Thanássis' speciality is *kebab*, a variation of souvláki where mincemeat is blended with onion and spices. The side dish of chili peppers will blow your head off. Open noon–late. Cash only.

OMONIA

Athinaïkon €€ *Themistokléous 2, metro Omónia, tel: 210 38 38 485.* This *ouzerí*, founded in 1932 but installed here in the early 1990s, is famous for its seafood *mezédes* like mussels *saganáki*, paella and fried *gávros* (anchovy). Classy décor, and efficient service. Busy at lunch with local business people. Closed Sun and Aug. Cash only.

Meet Me €€€ *Athinas 65, metro Omónia, tel: 210 32 50 900.* On the ground floor of the Baby Grand, the restaurant is as relaxed and as fun as the hotel itself. It serves superior versions of standard taverna dishes such as souvláki, chops, baked peppers and country sausages, but the quality is excellent and the prices reasonable. There's an affordable wine list too. Booking recommended. Open daily 7–11am, 1pm–1am.

Klimatariá €€ *Platía Théatrou 2, metro Omónia, tel: 210 32 16 629, www.klimataria.gr.* The *Klimatariá* is an excellent source of hearty, mostly meat-based cooking – as the row of *gástres*, the traditional stewing apparatus of mountain shepherds, tips you off as you enter. There are vegetarian and fish choices too, and great live acoustic music, a world away from 'Greek Night' travesties. Open Mon–Sat supper, plus Fri–Sun lunch. Cash only.

PANGRATI

O Karavítis €€ *Arktínou 33 and Pafsaníou 4, tel: 210 72 15 155.* *O Karavítis* is Pangráti's last surviving classic 1930s taverna, relying on baked casseroles, a few *mezédes* and grills, all washed down with bulk wine from the Mesógia (inland Attica). Traditional desserts like quince or semolina helva are available; outdoor seating in a lovely garden across the street. Supper only. Cash only.

O Kóstas € *Ekális 7, tel: 210 701 1101.* This decades-old little *koutoúki* (neighbourhood local) moved to this converted 1920s house around the millennium, preserving its brief menu featuring meatballs, sardines and bean soup, its popular prices and its loyal clientele. If anything, the cooking is even better, with Kostas' son-in-law now mostly in charge. Only about 30 seats indoors and on the terrace, so reserve at weekends. Supper only; closed Sun and Aug. Cash only.

Spondí €€€€€ *Pýrronos 5, tel: 210 75 20 658, www.spondi.gr.* With the kitchen under the command of a French chef, Michelin-starred Spondí – one of just three such restaurants in the city – is great for special occasions, with seating in a neoclassical house and its courtyard. Creative, often improbable, fusion cuisine combines continental and Pacific influences in herb- or truffle-flavoured duck, meat and fish dishes followed by decadent dessert concoctions prepared under the supervision of a Parisian patisserie. Closed lunch and Aug.

PLAKA

Ta Bakaliarákia (tou Damígou) €€ *Kydathinéon Street 41, metro Akrópoli, tel: 210 32 25 084.* This last surviving basement *koutoúki* in the area has décor seemingly unchanged since it was founded in 1865 (except for a photo of Josephine Baker eating here in the 1930s), and has been used as a retro film location. The barrels here hold good retsina, and of course the *bakaliarákia* (cod with garlic sauce) is the big attraction, though there are other typical dishes like hand-cut potatoes. Supper only except Sun, closed summer. Cash only.

Kóstas € *Adrianoú 116, metro Monastiráki, no phone.* A hole-in-the-wall *souvláki* booth with no tables or chairs, *Kóstas* serves succulent grilled souvláki in pitta bread with all the trimmings: the perfect snack while strolling through the district. Kóstas' daughter and son-in-law run the business now. Open Mon–Sat. Cash only.

Ouzeri Kouklis €€€ *Tripodon 14, metro Monastiráki, tel: 210 32 47 605.* This back-street Plaka place has been in the same family since 1935, and it's as popular as ever. In the evenings you might have to wait for a table, especially on the balcony overlooking the street. There's no menu, you simply choose from the trays of meze that the waiters bring to your table, and the very reasonable fixed price also includes a beer or half-bottle of wine. Open daily 11am–2am.

O Plátanos €€–€€€ *Diogénous 4, metro Monastiráki, tel: 210 32 20 666.* Facing a square near the Tower of the Winds shaded by a *plátanos* (plane tree), this small taverna founded in 1932 focuses on meaty stews and *laderá* (vegetable casseroles). The barrelled retsina is exceptional, and has been featured in wine guides as an example of what it should be like. Closed Sun night and Aug. Cash only.

PIRAEUS

Dourambeis €€€€ *Aktí Protopsálti Street 29, Piraeus/Páleo Fáliro border, tel: 210 41 22 092.* Cult seafood taverna *Dourambeis* has tasteful wood, stone and white-cloth décor. Starters like coarse-grained white *taramosaláta*, *saganáki* of razor clams, and fried crayfish nuggets can be better than the mains. Open lunch and dinner.

Vasílenas €€€€ *Etolikoú 72, Piraeus (Etolikoú runs north from Aktí Kondýli on the harbour), tel: 210 46 12 457.* Founder Thanássis

Vasílenas introduced the concept of set-price *table d'hôte* to Greece, captivating guests such as Sophia Loren, Mános Hatzidákis and Melína Mercoúri. His descendants continue the tradition, bringing 16 platters in sequence. The interior retains charming touches like old bottles and the marble serving counter. Supper only, closed Sun and Aug.

BEYOND ATHENS

Taverna Vakhos €€ *Apollonos 31, Delphi, tel: 22650 83186.* In Delphi many places cater for the tourist trade but this is a genuine local favourite, with hearty mountain fare like rooster or rabbit, and plenty of cheap local wine, too. It also has superb views if you can get there early and grab a good table. Open daily noon-late.

Kondylénia €€–€€€ *Kamínia, Ýdra (Hydra), tel: 22980 53520.* In addition to its unbeatable view over the sea, this taverna also serves good seafood – the grilled *thrápsalo* (sweet deep-water squid) is particularly recommendable. Open Lent–Oct 11am–late.

Ómorfo Tavernáki €€€ *Vassilísis Ólgas 16, Náfplio, tel: 27520 25944.* This taverna occupies a neoclassical building on one of the old town's narrower lanes. Its specialities include *kolokotroneïko* (pork in wine sauce) and *spetzofäï* (sausage and pepper stew). Tables both inside and on the lane. Closed midday summer Mon–Fri. Cash only.

Taverna Lazaros €€€ *Kastelli, Spétses Town, tel: 22980 72600.* If you stay on Spétses you have to have at least one meal at the Lazaros, but then you might never eat anywhere else. Terrific atmosphere, always crowded, and the food is cheap but exceptionally good taverna stuff. One house special is goat in lemon sauce. Cash only. Open daily from about 7pm until late. Closed winter.

Yeladhákis (aka tou Stéliou or Ily Agorá) €–€€ *Lane behind covered fish market, Égina town, tel: 22970 27308.* The first, best, and cheapest of the three rival seafood *ouzerís* on this lane. Accordingly, you may have to wait for a table as they don't take bookings. Their stock-in-trade is grilled octopus, sardines or shrimp. Cash only.

INDEX

Berlitz pocket guide

Athens

Twelfth Edition 2009

Written by Lindsay Bennett
Updated by Donna Dailey
Series Editor: Tony Halliday

Photography credits
All photography by Richard and Danielle
Nowitz, except: Ashmolean Museum 14;
Pete Bennett 34, 45, 55, 63, 69, 72;
Cyclades Museum 13; Marc Dubin 37;
Tony Halliday 36; Lebrecht 80; Topfoto
22; Bill Wassman 31

Cover picture: 4Corners Images

Printed in Singapore by Insight Print
Services (Pte) Ltd, 38 Joo Koon Road,
Singapore 628990. Tel: (65) 6865-1600.
Fax: (65) 6861-6438

Berlitz Trademark Reg. U.S. Patent Office
and other countries. Marca Registrada

Every effort has been made to provide
accurate information in this publication,
but changes are inevitable. The publisher
cannot be responsible for any resulting
loss, inconvenience or injury.

Contact us

At Berlitz we strive to keep our guides as
accurate and up to date as possible, but if you
find anything that has changed, or if you have
any suggestions on ways to improve this guide,
then we would be delighted to hear from you.

Berlitz Publishing, PO Box 7910,
London SE1 1WE, England.
fax: (44) 20 7403 0290
email: berlitz@apaguide.co.uk
www.berlitzpublishing.com